Diane Samuels

Diane Samuels was bor currently lives in Lond extensively as a playwrigh

Her play *Kindertransport*, first produced by Soho Theatre Company in 1993, won the Verity Bargate and Meyer-Whitworth Awards. It has been translated into many languages, and performed in the West End, Off-Broadway and all over the world. It was revived in 2007 by Shared Experience and in 2013 for a national tour by Hall and Childs. It is now studied at A and AS level, and is a set text for English Literature GCSE. Her other plays include *The True Life Fiction of Mata Hari* (Watford Palace Theatre, 2002); *Cinderella's Daughter* (Trestle Theatre tour, 2005); and *3 Sisters on Hope Street* (with Tracy-Ann Oberman), after Chekhov and inspired by the Jewish community of her upbringing (co-produced by Liverpool Everyman/Playhouse and Hampstead Theatre, 2008).

Her plays for younger audiences include *One Hundred Million Footsteps* for Quicksilver Theatre Company; *Chalk Circle, Frankie's Monster* (adapted from *The Monster Garden* by Vivien Alcock); and *How to Beat a Giant* at the Unicorn Theatre.

She has written many plays for BBC radio, including *Swine*, *Doctor Y*, *Watch Out for Mister Stork* and *Hen Party*. *Tiger Wings*, an original drama based on pilot Joan Allen's 1948 solo flight from England to Singapore, was broadcast as a five-part serial on BBC Radio 4 in 2012.

Diane has wide experience of teaching creative writing, lecturing at the universities of Birmingham, Reading, Oxford and Goldsmiths, and running workshops for IATE (Institute for Arts in Therapy and Education), Alternatives, Theatre Royal Haymarket and the National Gallery. She was Royal Literary Fund Fellow at the University of Westminster, 2008 to 2011, and visiting lecturer at Regent's University London from 2013. She runs a regular writers' group for adults at her home and is writer-in-residence at Grafton Primary School in Islington, North London.

Diane was one of a creative team awarded a Science on Stage and Screen Award by the Wellcome Trust in 2001. The resulting work, *PUSH*, was performed at the People Show Studios in London in 2003. Her short story, *Rope*, was broadcast as one of the 2002 winners of BBC Radio 4's online short-story competition, and in 2011 she wrote and recorded *Essay: Inter-rail Postcards* for BBC Radio 3. As Pearson Creative Research Fellow 2004/5 at the British Library, she completed research into magic, and her booklet *A Writer's Magic Notebook* was published in 2006.

Musical theatre includes the book and lyrics for *Persephone* (*a love story*), with composer/lyricist Maurice Chernick, and the book for *The A–Z of Mrs P*, tracing the creation of the London A–Z street guide, with music and lyrics by Gwyneth Herbert (Southwark Playhouse, 2014).

For more information visit www.dianesamuels.com.

Enquiries about creative-writing workshops and *Kindertransport* talks/workshops to dianesamuels@mac.com.

DIANE SAMUELS'

Kindertransport

The Author's Guide to the Play

NICK HERN BOOKS

London

www.nickhernbooks.co.uk

A Nick Hern Book

Diane Samuels' Kindertransport – Page to Stage
first published in Great Britain in 2014
as a paperback original by Nick Hern Books Limited,
The Glasshouse, 49a Goldhawk Road, London W12 8QP

Diane Samuels' Kindertransport – Page to Stage
copyright © 2014 Diane Samuels

Page to Stage series
copyright © 2014 Nick Hern Books Limited

Diane Samuels has asserted her right to be identified
as the author of this work

Cover photograph © Colin Willoughby/ArenaPAL:
Julia Malewski as Eva and Sian Thomas as Helga in the
1996 Vaudeville Theatre production of *Kindertransport*

Designed and typeset by Nick Hern Books, London
Printed and bound in Great Britain by
CPI Group (UK) Ltd

A CIP catalogue record for this book is available
from the British Library

ISBN 978 1 84842 284 1

Contents

Acknowledgements

Since my play *Kindertransport* was introduced as a text for study on A level, AS level and more recently GCSE exam syllabuses in the UK, I have travelled up and down the country to give talks or deliver writing and drama workshops on the play. I have often been touched and inspired by the insights, writing, questions and care with which students respond. Particular thanks to teachers Katie Ogilvie, formerly of St Benet Biscop High School, Bedlington, Northumberland; Louisa Connolly at Sacred Heart High School, Newcastle; Teresa Davey and Jill Haves at Manchester High School for Girls; and Sarah Baker and Nadine Winspur at St Martin in the Fields High School for Girls, Lambeth, London. Extracts from their students' work, both creative writing and considered essays, are included to illustrate different kinds of responses to the play.

Many, many thanks to all who have given their time to speak honestly and openly about their experience: actors Diana Quick (Evelyn), Lily Bevan (Faith), Matti Houghton (Eva), Eileen O'Brien (Lil), Marion Bailey (Evelyn), Alexi Kaye Campbell (The Ratcatcher), Ruth Mitchell (Helga), Sarah Shanson (Eva), Pandora Colin (Helga), Jane Kaczmarek (Helga), directors Abigail Morris and Polly Teale, and composer Peter Salem. It is also fortunate that a new production is in progress as I write this book and I had access to director Andrew Hall and designer Juliet Shillingford in the throes of working out how to mount the work, bringing a fresh and vital perspective too. Also, I am hugely grateful to Rena Gamsa, a refugee who came to England from Germany as a child in the 1930s, and Ruth Barnett, one of the Kinder, who have generously shared their life stories.

Many thanks to the audience members, readers and students who have written to me over the years to share their feelings and thoughts evoked by their encounters with the play, revealing their own life experiences.

Special thanks to Simon Garfield for his continued support, and, for their professional back-up, skill, vision and encouragement, to Nick Hern, Matt Applewhite, and editor Robin Booth of Nick Hern Books, and to my agent Caroline Underwood at Alan Brodie Representation. For their continuing love and encouragement, a big thank-you to Ben and Jake Garfield, and Paul Berrill.

*

The author and publisher gratefully acknowledge permission to quote extracts from the following:

Collected Poems by Karen Gershon and *We Came As Children: A Collective Autobiography of Refugees* edited by Karen Gershon, published by Papermac.

I Came Alone: The Stories of the Kindertransports edited by Bertha Leverton and Shmuel Lowensohn, published by Book Guild Publishing Ltd.

No Time to Say Goodbye, produced by Rapid Pictures, directed by Sally George.

A Tug on the Thread by Diana Quick. Reproduced with the kind permission of Little, Brown Book Group and David Higham Associates.

*

The playtext of *Kindertransport* by Diane Samuels is published by Nick Hern Books (second edition, 2008, ISBN 978 1 85459 527 0), and can be purchased with a discount from www.nickhernbooks.co.uk.

Introduction

'I can understand myself only in the light of inner happenings.'
Carl Jung

'People are trapped in history, and history is trapped in them.'
James Baldwin

Memory is unpredictable. Sometimes it forms clear as crystal. At other times it splinters into shards that refuse to fit together. Some pieces may connect whilst others remain elusive. Often, memories dissolve into a mist or vanish altogether into a sea of darkness, but this doesn't mean that they are no longer there. *Kindertransport* is a play in which invisible memory is made not only visible but material and physical, a living, breathing thing: a bedtime moment, a box of papers, a girl's hand clutching a crinkled photograph. If you think that you know what memory means, then the play asks you to think again, to feel, see, hear, touch where memory hides and reveals itself, to realise that the value of what you do and do not remember might not lie in the past but in how it connects you to what is fully alive, or solidly frozen, within you right now, as present as ever.

Collective memory crystallises into what we call History. 'Facts' serve to anchor the shared story into a generally agreed narrative. The 'objective' and relevant facts that provide the wider context for this play start in Germany in the late 1930s.

In early November 1938, an intensive series of 'pogrom' attacks on Jewish property and arrests of people were launched in Nazi Germany. This became known as Kristall-nacht ('The Night of Broken Glass'), and has subsequently been called Pogromnacht or Novemberpogrome. In the wake of this calculated violence, some others in the world woke up to the level of danger that certain minorities, most notably Jews, faced within the Nazi domain. The British government was lobbied by Jewish, humanitarian and Quaker organisations to provide refuge. At the time, it was not necessarily easy but certainly possible for people to get out of Germany, surrendering their possessions in the process. The difficulty was finding somewhere to go when many countries were barring their doors to refugees no matter how endangered they were. The ten thousand permits that were made available for under-sixteen-year-olds to enter and remain within the United Kingdom were hard won and granted only because children were seen as less of a threat to the economy, which was still recovering from the ravages of the Great Depression. So, at the very end of 1938, began a series of transportations carrying mostly Jewish children (along with some from other backgrounds who were also at risk) aged sixteen and under from Germany, Austria and Czechoslovakia. The name these transportations were given is simply descriptive – Kinder ('children'), transport ('transportation'). These continued for almost a year until the Second World War began in early September 1939.

It was in 1989, during the fiftieth anniversary year of the Kindertransport, that I first learned about these children who were brought to safety, and how many of them never saw their parents again. I wondered why I had not come across this before. I grew up in a tight-knit Jewish community in Liverpool in the 1960s and '70s, and attended Jewish schools from kindergarten at the age of three to secondary school, including sixth form. I was taught Jewish history and the Holocaust was given due attention. Yet there was no word about the Kindertransport, and this in schools where young people of the same age would readily have identified with the experience of these evacuees. The reasons for this are significant and connect with the inner life of the Kinder themselves. Many simply chose not to discuss or raise the matter of where they had come from and how. In their adult lives they had focused on making a living, raising families and 'putting the past behind' them. When the 1989 anniversary came around, the youngest Kinder, who had travelled across Europe and the North Sea as babies thrust into the arms of older children, were themselves in their fifties, whilst the teenage refugees were in their sixties. Late middle-age is a time when life catches up with a person. An organisation called Kindertransport Reunion was set up by Bertha Leverton and others who now actively sought to mark the event by bringing as many Kinder together as possible. A celebratory gathering was planned, the first of its kind. I met Bertha through a friend, herself a refugee, of my then husband, himself the son of German Jewish refugees. She talked to me about arriving and living in England, then later, after the war, how her mother had been one of the few who survived and had come to find her. Bertha also helped me to meet other Kinder and hear their stories too. I watched a documentary on television in which a number of them described their early experience of escape, subsequent survival, gratitude, guilt, loss and making a new life in another land.

Twenty-five years on, 2013/14 sees the seventy-fifth anniversary. Kinder gather again to mark their unique experience and connect with each other. By the time the hundredth anniversary arrives it is unlikely that very many, if any, will be here to attend. I feel privileged to have been able to engage with this communal act of remembering, reflection and attesting to the world whilst many have still been here to share it.

Kindertransport, the event, is entirely distinct from *Kindertransport* the play. In the drama I do not attempt to speak for any of those who actually travelled on the trains as children. Whilst I did draw on key moments and detail from the spoken and written testimonies of Kinder, and whilst most of the experiences of Eva/Evelyn (the principal character in my play, played by two actors at different stages of her life) did happen to someone somewhere, the play is primarily a work of creative imagination, written from the heart. My play does focus on a particular happening at a time of massive upheaval in the world, yet it also looks beyond the specifics of this historical event and taps into a universal human experience: that of a child's separation from its mother.

This book is intended to share my reflections on the creating and telling of Eva/Evelyn's story, how it relates to historical events both personal and political, the way it works theatrically and what I have learned over the years about audience and readership responses. Giving unique insight into each character are a few of the actors who have played them, lived inside their skins. Providing their specific takes on music, design and realising the text in production are a composer, designer and three different directors who have worked on a number of key productions over the years: the world premiere at the Cockpit Theatre in 1993, produced by the Soho Theatre Company, directed by Abigail Morris; the production, also directed by Abigail Morris, that transferred from the Palace Theatre, Watford, to the Vaudeville Theatre in London's West End, in 1996; Shared Experience's national touring production, directed by Polly Teale, in the UK in 2007; and the national UK tour for 2013/14, directed by Andrew Hall, produced by Hall and Childs. It has been fascinating to catch up again with them all and a revelation to discover how their lives have been touched in some meaningful way by this story.

Most of all, my focus when writing the play was to probe the inner life where memory is shaped by trauma, history meets story, in order to gain psychological and emotional insight into how a damaged psyche can survive, possibly recover, and whether there might ever be an opportunity to thrive. This journey within is what *Kindertransport* also offers each member of the audience and reader if they allow themselves to go where it ventures, no matter where or when they live.

Cover of the first edition of *Kindertransport*,
Nick Hern Books, 1995

Background

'Dear Ms Samuels, I enjoyed your play very much. It has given me a whole different perspective on how I look at mother/daughter relationships. If you don't mind me asking – how did you feel when you were putting all of this together?'
Email enquiry from student

'Imagination and fiction make up more than three-quarters of our real life.' *Simone Weil*

Fiction writers are often asked if their stories are autobiographical.

Fiction... a thing feigned or imaginatively invented... pretence... a thing created.

Shorter Oxford English Dictionary, 5th Edition, 2002

No matter how a play or novel is 'invented', it certainly comes from something very alive for the author. The essence of the themes, characters, images, moments, is without doubt inspired by personal experience in some way. What is 'make-believe' tends often to reflect an aspect of inner 'fantasy', 'imaginative' or 'dream' states even if it says nothing about actual life experience. 'Is your story autobiographical?' is one of those seemingly straightforward but rather confounding questions, like 'Who are you?', to which you might first respond with your name but, on greater reflection, double take: 'Is this who I really am?' Is the name that you were given at birth or have adopted somewhere along the way, the place you were born, the class or race or gender that you inherit, the shape of your body, the talents you possess, the faults you hide, the mistakes you make, a definer of who you are? Who chooses a person's customs, accent, attitude, character, history? 'Who am I?'

is a question that secretly haunts Evelyn in *Kindertransport* and it is so unnerving for her that she refuses to face it. So, my answer to whether *Kindertransport* is in any way autobiographical is, in all honesty, 'No, and yes', or, if I think again, 'Yes, and no', especially as, in this case, the process of making the play involved tapping into the stuff of life to invent the drama.

> *Autobiography...* The writing of one's own history; a story of a person's life written by him or herself.
>
> *Autobiographical...* relating to one's own life story.
>
> *Biography...* The history of the lives of individuals, as a branch of literature.
>
> *Art...* the production of a work of imagination, imitation, or design, or towards the gratification of the aesthetic senses: the products of any such pursuit.
>
> *Shorter Oxford English Dictionary, 5th Edition, 2002*

Given my family and cultural background, it would seem that *Kindertransport* is in no way autobiographical. My own mother was not a refugee from Nazi Germany. She was born and raised in North West England in the genteel Lancashire seaside resort of Southport by a mother who was born in Liverpool and a father who grew up in Llandudno, another seaside resort, in North Wales. My father is a born-and-bred native of Liverpool, as was his mother, whilst his father was born in Russia and was brought by his parents to Liverpool when he was a baby. My great-grandparents on both sides emigrated from Russia and Poland at the beginning of the twentieth century, before the First World War, to Britain. So, whilst my family are Jews, none of them experienced the Holocaust directly.

German Jewish culture in the nineteenth and early twentieth centuries was quite distinct from that of Polish and Russian Jews. Whilst German culture did maintain an implicit antagonism towards Jews, those living in Germany could at least be educated, climb the social ladder and were given the opportunity to integrate, up to a point, into wider society. In Russia and Poland, anti-Semitism was blatant and the opportunity for integration was most certainly not on offer. Jews were kept separate from the mainstream, isolated in an area called The Pale of Settlement, which included a few large cities, like Odessa and Kiev, with many living in shtetls (rural villages or towns). One of the consequences of being kept apart was that, within their own communities, Jews lived without cultural compromise, speaking their own language, Yiddish (an amalgamation of German and Hebrew), in an environment run according to Jewish traditions. German Jews, on the other hand, more readily adopted German customs and ways of behaving, spoke 'proper' German and, for fear of being different, a target for discrimination or prejudice, would play down their Jewish practices and ways, adapt their Jewish identity if this was possible, or let it slip altogether.

There is a tension in what it was like to be a German Jew that resonates with the question of 'Who am I?' For if, as a member of a minority group, you are forever fearful that you won't get on in the world if you fully express your ethnic and religious culture, and if you are careful to temper or hide it, well then: who are you? Are you who you appear to be on the outside, or are you what you inherit from your culture and 'ancestors', much of which is concealed? Are you one person or two – someone who is 'out' and someone else who is 'in'? This split sense of self certainly informs the development of the character of Evelyn and roots her in the cultural background of a German Jewish way of operating that precedes her separation from her original family.

What if the question 'Who am I?' was posed within Eva's family on the eve of her leaving Hamburg in early 1939? Would Helga, her mother, say of herself that she was a German Jew, or even a Jewish German, when many Germans at the time were refusing to acknowledge that a Jew was a human being, let alone of the same nationality?

What about asking: 'Who am I not?'

Often a writer is driven to call on what they have never directly experienced. It is as if the imagination strives to embrace something outside yourself in an attempt to add a missed dimension by conjuring it in a virtual reality. I was raised in a community that resembled in some ways those shtetls of Eastern Europe from which my family originated. Everyone I mixed closely with on a social level, in school, in synagogue, in communal settings, was Jewish. They peppered their English with Yiddish and Hebrew, observed the festivals and identified strongly as Jews in the outside world. This was the template that for some reason my imagination felt compelled to reverse. Thus I found myself creating a character who is not me at all, and in being 'not me' is the part of me that I am possibly afraid of being – a Jew who is cut off from all other Jews, purposefully concealing all remaining traces of her Jewishness, like a rotting corpse buried beneath the attic floorboards, to become anything but a Jew – in Evelyn's case an English Christian.

With regards to my own situation at the time of writing *Kindertransport*, something significant was certainly happening that must have informed my being drawn so strongly to the experience of the Kinder. The fiftieth-anniversary reunion in 1989, when I began the research, led to my writing in earnest in 1990/91. In 1988 my first child was born, and my second arrived two years later in 1990. So, autobiographical? Well, 'Yes, and no.' *Kindertransport* focuses on the relationships between generations of mothers and daughters, whereas both my children are sons. A film producer once asked, 'Why are there only women in this play, bar the Ratcatcher, who isn't a person?' I glibly joked that I was at the time living in a household with three men of varying ages and needed to dream up some kind of feminine environment. Short of having another baby in the hope that it might be a daughter, I concocted the female world that I lacked. Life in reverse again.

Becoming a mother made me acutely aware of the constant struggle between what a mother can and can't do to cater fully for the needs of her child. Writing after disturbed nights, between feeds and naps, tuned me in to some very basic emotions. I was at times fulfilled and at other times overwhelmed by the love and sense of responsibility, concerned about not being a good enough mother. I worked hard not to let down these little people whose lives relied upon me and in whom I couldn't help but invest more than I dared admit. I also had a strong sense that my primary job was to encourage my sons to be themselves and to raise them to manage independently. More profoundly, it gave me direct experience twice over within two years of the rawest and most seminal parting that every single human being on the planet experiences – birth itself. In labour, a woman has no choice but to let go, in violent spasms, of the new life she has been protecting. For both mother and child this is a wrench and a release. We have all been there one way or another, expelled from the womb, the contained world inside, out into the uncontained world beyond. It is the very first moment of 'Who am I?', no longer part of another but a separate person in our own right. This is one of the most profound shifts that any of us ever experience and we carry it submerged within ourselves for our entire lives.

'What's an abyss, Mutti?' asks Eva of Helga the night before she is sent away on one of the trains.

'An abyss is a deep and terrible chasm.'

In the first two lines of the play, here is the heart of the whole piece in a nutshell: what is this gap, Mummy, and why have we been split apart when we were together as one?

Shall we make ourselves forget and never fully acknowledge how we feel about this primary experience of leaving 'home'? Or do we need ways of embracing the sense of loss that lies at the heart of the human condition, and isn't art in any form – music, literature, dance, painting, sculpture, photography, poetry and theatre – a way of 'going there', to those raw feelings, safely?

In this raw state, as a new mother, in 1989, a friend told me about her father's anticipation of the fiftieth-anniversary reunion of those on the Kindertransport. I wasn't aware of the transportations, let alone that there was an anniversary at hand. My friend explained that her father had escaped from Vienna on one of the trains when he was seventeen, using fake papers because he was above the permitted age limit of sixteen. The way she described this event buzzed with personal significance, as if it mattered to her as much as it did her father. Then I recalled that she had revealed once how she needed regularly to check where her passport was, just in case. I'd fleetingly thought this strange. I tend to dig out my passport the night before leaving the country and forget about it when it's not imminently required. How many people do feel an insistent urge to locate their identifying documents on a weekly basis? There seemed to be a connection between the flight that her father had had to make in his teens and a disquiet in her, as if she too may need to escape without warning. This was not based on any direct threat of danger in her own life. She had grown up in a comfortable middle-class home just outside London, had been very successful as a student, and at the time lived safely in her own flat in North London. She had never been threatened with expulsion, imprisonment or a direct attack on any of her citizen's rights. I sensed that something about her father's experience had been directly inherited by her, and she was expressing a nagging inner state of insecurity often experienced by those described as 'second generation', the children of survivors or refugees.

Then, an old friend of my then husband's family, herself a German Jewish refugee who came to Britain with her family after Hitler came to power, shared the confusion that she had experienced when she first went to school in Britain without knowing a word of English. She was all at sea in this alien world and was grateful to be taught a smattering of words by her fellow classmates, who tricked her into saying silly or embarrassing things, provoking confusion or much amusement, until she worked out that she was the victim of a practical joke. In her sixties, the experience of being unable to communicate and prey to ridicule still carried a sting as she reminisced more articulately than most native speakers in beautifully coined English.

That year I also attended the 'shiva house' of another friend, whose father had died suddenly. In Jewish tradition, for the week after the funeral, the close kin of the deceased 'sit shiva', in mourning, as friends, wider family and the community visit them at home. My friend, struggling to come to terms with the loss, still in shock, revealed that his mother had been sitting only a day or two earlier with one of her oldest friends and they'd begun to discuss their experience together during the war. This was unusual, unheard of. His mother never talked about her childhood in Europe, merely hinted that she'd been in hiding somewhere or other. It was a taboo subject. Yet here she was suddenly recalling in some detail what she and her friend had gone through in the concentration camp of Auschwitz. Her son and daughter had grown up knowing nothing about this major experience of their mother's. They were being let in to her early life for the first time.

I wondered how these things fitted together. The questions began to unfold:

- If a child can inherit psychological states, and emotional and physical experience, from a parent as markedly as he or she can inherit genetic characteristics, then what if these experiences are hidden?

- What does a fear or a dirty secret or a wound do to a child when they don't know it's there in their parent and yet their lives are being deeply informed by it?

- How much and in what ways can a parent hide their experience from their children?

- What is behind the urge to hide what has happened and how does this affect who you are to yourself and others?

- What if you even hide yourself from yourself?

Then I watched a documentary commemorating the Kinder-transport on TV. In *No Time to Say Goodbye*, made by Rapid Pictures, directed by Sally George, a number of Kinder in 1989 (no longer children at all, of course, but adults in their fifties and sixties) spoke with remarkable candour about their experience as a Kind (the singular of the German word Kinder, i.e. 'child'). One woman interviewed in the documentary explained how she had, in her twenties, thirties and forties focused on day-to-day living and getting on with her life. She had felt no desire to dwell upon her experience of leaving her family behind in Germany and coming to England on the trains as a child. She saw herself as remarkably fortunate to have been spared the sufferings of those left behind in Europe and was grateful to her parents for having the foresight to send her to safety. She was one of the lucky ones. Then, as she reached her fifties, she entered a different phase of her life:

> The turning point for me was in this very room actually. My son had left, grown up and gone to college, moved away. My [adoptive] mother had died. My husband had left. All my roles had gone, and here I was hoovering one day, feeling enormously solitary and lonely. At that very time I was on a counselling course doing my counselling training. So as this stuff was emerging in me I actually had somewhere to take it, and that is not chance, that I was in the right place at the right time. That's when I began to lift my defences and do my mourning. I had not done any grieving until that time. I was forever strong and cheerful.

> I remember pulling up on Highgate Hill one night and needing to get out as the rage overtook me and the feeling was, 'How dare you send me away and get yourselves killed?' And then came the tears. The joy of crying. Actually allowing the tears out. That was my liberation.

Watching the film, I asked myself what I would do as a parent in such a situation. What if my own family was in mortal danger, the threat increasingly imminent? What if an opportunity were to arise to send my children to a foreign country where they would be safe? Could I, would I send my sons, still so young, away?

In my gut I knew what I'd do. I would do what this woman's parents did. Ask any parent whether they would send their child away from peril to safety and most parents may not relish the choice but they say that they would do this. But the child within me knew what my children would want. Ask any child if they would rather be sent away to safety or stay with their family in danger, under threat of starvation, brutality or death. In my experience, every child without exception, every adult remembering their own childhood feelings, does not hesitate to say that they'd want with all their being to be with their family, and prefer to die with them.

At the end of the play Evelyn faces Helga with the swallowed, 'shameful' truth at last:

> EVELYN....I never wanted to live without you and you made me...

This is the profound question and contradiction that lies at the heart of *Kindertransport*: what happens when the parent's survival instinct is directly in opposition to what the child profoundly needs? There is no easy solution. Somehow the impossibility of this conflict must be borne. But how and at what price?

Cover of the second edition of *Kindertransport*,
Nick Hern Books, 2008

Life Stories

'It was an ordinary train
travelling across Germany
which gathered and took us away
those who saw it may have thought
that it was for a holiday
not being exiled being taught
to hate what we had loved in vain
brought us lasting injury'

Karen Gershon, 'The Children's Exodus', from Collected Poems

Eva/Evelyn in *Kindertransport* is not a particular person who really existed. I imagined her into being. To do this authentically, it was essential to find out more from those who had actually come over to Britain on the Kindertransport about what had happened, physically and emotionally, in specific detail.

There is a view that History consists of the stories constructed about the past by the 'victors', or current mainstream culture, to justify the status quo, maintain it in the present and into the future – all that emphasis on kings, presidents, wars, religious movements, economic 'progress'. I studied History at university and spent much of my first two years reading the work of historians writing about other historians' writing about yet more historians' ideas and interpretations of many a grand narrative. Then, in my third year, I was given the opportunity to complement this 'secondary' material by studying some primary, first-hand source material. There is something charged about the stuff that comes from a time and place, connecting with the people living the experience there and then. Recently, when I was attached to the British Library as Pearson Creative Research Fellow, I was taken into the vaults below St Pancras by one of the curators. He pulled off the shelf a copy of Anne Boleyn's Bible. Inside were her handwritten notes. Knowing that this belonged to the figure whose place in the big story of British History has so often been told certainly contributed to my sense of awe at encountering her personal possession. Yet also in this moment, when I touched the holy book that she had long ago touched, and saw her handwriting, I felt her as a woman simply holding a pen and writing, reading, praying. An entirely different dimension was added to my sense of what History is, and this was to do with the small things in life which somehow resonate with the big things. As a child I always loved visiting old buildings, the older the better, and I sensed vividly the layers of generations living with their different customs and preoccupations in the same spot where I was standing. All around are the fragments in the physical environment of earlier lives. These can take the form of letters, songs, photographs, paving stones, railings, pictures, plates, vases, shoes – anything. It is up to those who are here now, all survivors one way or another, to notice the clues, honour the struggles, successes, failures, courage, cowardice, uniqueness and ordinariness that informs the world we inhabit. For it is the survivors who mark History, and we can choose to tell it as a story or we can evoke it as a mosaic by piecing together the fragments to create a composite picture that at once embraces and re-envisages many different facets all at once.

One of the joys of working with events that happened within living memory is that those who lived them can speak directly and address whatever questions you may have. This gives access not only to the physical experience but to something of the inner life, the intangible part of a person, too.

The very first interview that I conducted was with the old friend of my then husband's family, who had already shared smatterings of her life story over family meals on visits to her home in Hendon, North West London. Rena Gamsa was more than happy to tell me about coming to London in the

1930s from Hamburg in Germany as a child. Her immigration preceded the Kindertransport by a few years. Her family was able to leave Germany together before the situation further deteriorated. Rena gave me some insight into what it is to flee to a strange place when your country of birth can no longer be a safe home. She remembered clearly how it was to start to settle down into a new home when you are perceived to be and feel like a foreigner. Some of what Rena told me has found its way into Eva's experience. When I first interviewed her in 1990, I took handwritten notes. In the summer of 2013, I invited Rena, now in her nineties, to write down her testimony in her own words.

> I was born in Hamburg, Germany. Like my mother and aunts, I went to a Jewish girls' school. My brother and I, like most of our friends, had a nanny who took us out to the parks where we often met our friends. In the winter we always had a lot of snow, so we used to go to the park with our toboggan, or to the frozen Alster [a lake where the River Alster flows through Hamburg] to skate. For the whole of the summer, my parents had a flat by the sea, where we went with our nanny, and our parents and their friends came at weekends. My parents had a large circle of friends, and they seemed to be always busy entertaining.

> My best friend lived in the same block of flats as we did. She was not Jewish, but we were great friends. One day her brother came in his Hitler Youth uniform, and told my friend that she must not play with me any more, as I was a 'Dirty Jew'. He then spat at me and pulled her away. Later her parents came to see my parents to apologise, but said that we must not see each other again. They were frightened that their son would tell his teacher and they would be in trouble.

> Soon after, Hitler came to power. He came to visit Hamburg. We were told to welcome him, but to stay on our balcony. Hitler and his henchmen came in an open-top car, and the crowd went mad. It was absolute mass hysteria, and frightened me stiff. I have always had a fear of crowds since then. I also had nightmares for some time.

When I was eleven, my brother and I were told by my parents that we were going on a lovely holiday, but not to tell anyone. I knew that something was up when all sorts of new bits of furniture and other things arrived; we were told that they had decided to renew some of the old things. My mother bought me all sorts of clothes that were much too big for me, 'Because there is a sale on.' Since I saw no sale signs anywhere, I guessed this was part of the 'special holiday'.

We came to England on a big ship on the Hamburg America line. In those days the big liners could not get into Southampton, so we were taken off the ship onto a small boat. Before this, the Germans went though all our papers very thoroughly. My parents were very nervous. When we landed in Southampton, my parents hugged each other, 'We are free.' This was on 1st March 1935. When we entered the train to London, I was very concerned that we could not go into the apartment that said 'Smoking'. In German, 'smoking' meant a dinner-jacket suit and my father was not wearing one.

We were met by my father's sister and brother-in-law, who had come to England eighteen months before us. They lived in Sydenham in South East London, and we stayed with them for a while.

We arrived in England on a Friday, and I was sent to school on Monday. As I did not speak one word of English, my three boy cousins said that they would teach me just a few words: every time the teacher smiles at you, you must get up, curtsy and say, 'Yes', which in English is 'No'; then I must say, 'Thank you very much', which in English is 'You are a blooming nuisance'. The class, after the initial shock, fell about laughing. I thought that they were just being nice to me. Since I could not speak one word of English, no one could make me understand. In the end they called my father to come and collect me. Needless to say I was horrified and refused to go back to school. The Headmistress then introduced me to one of my classmates who took care of me and became my best friend. It was her family that taught me English.

I loved going to school and loved the sports that we played, as in German schools in those days we had no sports.

They were more interested in me being Jewish, as in that part of London there were very few Jews. One day the Headmistress called me in to tell me that a new pupil was coming to our school, and although she was older than me, I should look after her. I did not like her and she was very reluctant to have anything to do with me. She left after a term to go back to Germany. I suspected that she was a spy.

When the war broke out, my father, along with most men over sixteen, was interned as an Enemy Alien. He was taken to a camp in Huyton where they had to walk from the station to the camp. All along the route the local people came out and shouted, 'Heil Hitler! You bloody Germans.' No one understood that we Jews were the country's most loyal people.

He was only in the camp for six weeks. We Enemy Aliens had to get rid of our radios and our maps and atlases. Luckily our neighbours (my best friend's parents) took all our things for safe keeping and so that we could hear what was going on. They took our radio and put it on the fence in our garden, so that we could listen to the news. One day the police arrived and told us to stay in the living room while they searched the house. No reason was given. When they came back to us they apologised and said that one of our neighbours had reported that we, the Germans, were signalling the planes. Nothing was found, and our blackout was in perfect order. I still speak German, but think in English.

Rena knew Bertha Leverton, one of the key figures who set up the Kindertransport Reunion organisation and the fiftieth-anniversary get-together. When I met and interviewed her in 1989, Bertha, along with co-editor Shmuel Lowensohn, was also gathering testimonies from as many Kinder as she could find for a book, *I Came Alone: The Stories of the Kindertransports*. In this book, she includes an introduction explaining its purpose.

One day, in June 1988, I realised that it was forty-nine years ago that I had come to this country, and looked in vain for any sign of a commemoration to be held for our forthcoming fiftieth jubilee. Also, looking at my grandchildren, one of whom was exactly the same age as I on leaving Germany, made me think and realise what our parents and relatives must have felt to let their children go.

Whilst Bertha's parents did survive and came to find her after the war, she confirms that most of the Kinder lost their parents in the Holocaust and never saw them again. Bertha and her brother, who escaped with her, also suffered ill-treatment at the hands of their foster mother, whom they called Auntie. Reading the collection of recollections, I noticed the range of experience. Some children found themselves in loving homes, others in hostels, some in cities, others in remote rural areas, some with Jewish families, some with Christian ones, some with childless couples, some with large families. Yet there are similarities too, as Bertha attests.

If some of the stories seem repetitive, please realise that our experiences were often identical; for instance the journey, described so many times by so many of us, was a trauma, as was the realisation of having become orphans when the rest of the world celebrated victory.

Bertha put me in touch with some of the other Kinder whom I also interviewed, as well as the father of the friend who first told me about his going to the Reunion. I listened to and I read many testimonies. I absorbed. I imagined. Fragments of so many different 'true life' perspectives found their way into Eva's fictional tale.

Nearly everything Eva experiences did happen to someone somewhere.

Sometimes, these life-meets-art-meets-life moments in the drama are reflected back again by members of the audience when the play is in production. There is one scene in which Eva is caught by Lil, her English foster mother, having sneaked off to an affluent area of Manchester where she has been knocking on doors and asking the residents to employ her birth parents as domestic servants and sponsor them to come over to Britain. One evening, after the show, a woman came up to me and said: 'You know, that happened to me. I went out and I tried to get jobs for my parents. You got it so right.' I asked her for her name and it was the same woman whose testimony had initially inspired me to write the scene.

Ruth Barnett was also one of the many Kinder who came to see the first production of *Kindertransport* at the Cockpit Theatre in London in 1993.

> The first time I saw it I was just gobsmacked. I thought, 'That's practically my story.' It was so accurate.

Ruth has seen five or six different productions of the play over the years. 'Each time I see it I'm moved tremendously. I sort of see more.'

In 2013, I met and interviewed Ruth at her home in West Hampstead and asked whether any one child's experience can capture the essence of all the experiences.

> Kinder is plural. Kind is singular. I can't represent all the Kinder. We are so disparate. Everybody has a unique experience.

She travels the country giving talks in schools and brings to bear her own professional insight, having worked as a teacher and psychotherapist.

> I was born in Berlin in 1935, the year that the Nazis took citizenship away from all the Jews. So I was a person with no nationality by the time I was eight months old. That's why I have called my book *Person of No Nationality*. I had no nationality until I was eighteen and became British.

> My father was a judge in Berlin until he was sacked in 1933 by the Nazis. My mother was not Jewish. She ran his family cinema advertising business. She too was sacked in 1933 because they took away the business. I had a brother, three years older, called Martin. After Kristallnacht, 'The Night of Broken Glass', our parents arranged for us to go on the Kindertransport to England. I was four years old, my brother was seven.

> My mother was able to bring us on the train in February 1939 because she was an Aryan German citizen and could

get a holiday visa. She came with us but she had to go back. She wasn't Jewish and she would have been an enemy, not just an Enemy Alien, when war broke out. And at any rate she needed to go back and get my dad out. He left it till the last moment because his mum, my grandmother, was in hospital dying, and like so many other families, they wouldn't get out if they had elderly or ill relatives who couldn't travel. I found out that my grandmother didn't die till May 1939, so he really did leave it until the last moment, but he escaped to Shanghai and he survived there.

Our mother brought us to our first foster home with a vicar and his wife in Kent. They wanted us brought up Christian to protect us from anti-Semitism, which was rife in England. They were willing to take us both, which was very important. The whole world had disappeared except for my brother, and for him except for me, so we represented to each other a delicate thread of continuity, which is psychologically terribly important. Those Kinder who were totally cut off, on their own, that was a much harder experience to manage. People didn't realise at that time how important it was to keep siblings together; a lot were split up and had a rough time. But some had a good time.

Our foster father was an elderly, kindly, real English gentleman who I was very fond of. He was really nice, but his wife had no children and really didn't want other people's children foisted on her. She was very cruel. We were very unhappy in that first foster home, until the Quakers who sponsored us realised we were unhappy and sent us to a Quaker boarding school, which was wonderful.

After a couple of years our foster father died (I think he was already ill) and our foster mother refused to have us for the school holidays, which we were very pleased about. We were put in a hostel in London for displaced, bombed-out children, just homeless children, and there were scores of them. Nobody was unkind. It was unsupervised, and unhygienic. We both got very ill. I would have been about eight and Martin would have been eleven. We were still together. We had been very strictly supervised at the vicar's and at the school and suddenly there was no supervision. We weren't supposed to leave the property but it was in Richmond and we found our way down to the Thames. We swam in the Thames, because it was a hot summer, and Martin got hepatitis very badly and I sat and mopped his brow, and he had the idea that an apple a day keeps the doctor away, so I had to get some apples. Of course, we had no money. I sold my doll to a lady with a baby in the road and she gave me a few pennies and I got a big bag of apples. That was a morale boost. The apples didn't do it but it was the fact of us being together and hope. I got a tummy bug, I was very ill too. Oh and the kids had nits in their hair and the treatment for nits there was to dunk you in paraffin, and I came up in horrible blisters all round my neck. But we survived.

Then we found another foster family. The Quakers were responsible for us. The second family was also in Kent, a very different family with five children and they treated us exactly the same as their children. We were very happy there. But after two years the doodlebugs came over, and we were living in their path. They put guns all round where we were living to try to shoot them down, and they occasionally did shoot one down. I just found it exciting. But Martin, who was twelve or thirteen by then, he had a map in his mind. He knew where Germany was and he knew that his mother was there, which I didn't. And he experienced it as his mother throwing these awful bomb things directly at him, and he couldn't cope. He went berserk. So he had to be moved out of the path of the doodlebugs.

They found another family in Sussex, who would only take both children. So I had to go along as well, which was right but I didn't understand it. I was devastated at having to leave this lovely family and my buddy Joan, one of the girls. We were the same age, always together like twins. But I had to go along. I just thought that I was impossible, that nobody could cope with me for longer than a year or two and then they had to send me away. That's what kids understand, no matter what you tell them. I'm sure they explained to me, but it just went in one ear and out the other. I just experienced it as losing my buddy. A lot of loss.

The third foster family was a farm with four children and we settled in very quickly, and I was in seventh heaven with the animals. The war ended very soon after we came to the farm. But nothing changed. We had celebration parties and then life went on as usual. And four years went by after the war. I decided that I was going to leave school and be on the farm and raise animals. You could leave school at fourteen. That's what I was going to do.

Outline of the Play

'There is no doubt fiction makes a better job of the truth.'
Doris Lessing

'All sorrows can be borne if you put them in a story.'
Isak Dinesen

'A drama starts because a situation is imbalanced by a lie... At the end of the play the lie is revealed.' *David Mamet*

There are those stories that we tell often, so that the event almost gets left behind and the story of it takes over. Then there are stories that are never told. Did they even happen? Yet the sense of them pulsing inside won't go away. What is forgotten can be more potent than what is remembered. It throbs as a flush of warmth, a longing, an ache, a flutter of the heart, a quickening of the breath, a night terror. Everything we have been through lives in our bodies, sinews and blood. It is ingrained in our cells.

When unbearable experiences and wounding are buried, the impact they have on the present becomes more powerfully destructive and limiting. How can whatever has been experienced be faced and integrated into consciousness? In *Kindertransport*, a profound hidden trauma and the survivor's guilt that accompanies it are revealed, in an attempt to begin to find some measure of healing.

SETTING

The entire play is set in the mid-1980s in the attic of Evelyn's home in an outer London suburb, or perhaps in one of the Home Counties of South East England, like Surrey, Sussex or Kent.

Everything that occurs in the play takes place inside this attic, no matter what other times and places are also evoked.

CHARACTERS

EVELYN – a middle-class English woman in her fifties.

FAITH – Evelyn's only child, twenty years old.

EVA – nine-year-old German-Jewish girl who grows to be seventeen during the course of the play.

HELGA – German-Jewish woman, mother of Eva, initially in her early thirties and then around forty years old.

LIL – English working-class woman from Manchester who veers between her younger self in her mid-thirties and older self in her eighties.

THE RATCATCHER – mythical figure, musician, phantom, nightmare, who also plays: Nazi Border Official, English Organiser, Postman and Station Guard.

Act One

Scene One

Deep within an attic not far from London in the late twentieth century, sit a mother and daughter from another time and place: Hamburg, Germany, in early 1939. The mother, Helga Schlesinger, is instructing nine-year-old Eva to sew a button onto her new coat. Eva would prefer to have a bedtime story read to her from the book that she holds, entitled *Der Rattenfänger* (*The Ratcatcher*). Tomorrow, early, Eva is going away on a train that will take her to safety in England. The Schlesinger family are Jewish and, under the Nazi regime currently in power in Germany, their lives are threatened. With reined-in urgency, Helga presses Eva to continue with her packing.

Suddenly, in the 1980s, the door of the attic opens and Evelyn enters with her daughter Faith, in search of household objects that will be of use to Faith, who is about to leave home to live with her friends in a student flat share. Neither Evelyn nor Faith are aware of the presence of Helga and Eva who, in turn, are unaware of them. As the boxes are carefully opened and Evelyn offers fine china or silverware pieces that are not really suitable for student accommodation, Faith airs her doubts about moving out. It becomes apparent that Evelyn is divorced from Faith's father and Faith is concerned about leaving her mother to live alone. After a tense exchange, Faith changes her mind and decides not to leave after all and instead to stay at home for the time being. Evelyn closes the boxes, tells Faith to tidy up and leaves the attic.

As Eva and Helga continue to pack, Faith tentatively begins to explore the attic, opening boxes and looking inside each one.

Helga reveals to Eva that the cobbler has hidden inside the heels of her shoes some gold jewellery, including a watch and a Star of David on a chain, a travelling gift. She makes one final check of Eva's suitcase and finds a harmonica packed amongst the clothes. She chides Eva because it is forbidden to take anything of value out of Germany and she might be sent back if she is found with it. Still, when Helga's back is turned, Eva slips the harmonica back into her case before locking it tightly shut.

Faith has discovered a box of her childhood toys, dolls and a train set. The attic door opens. Lil, Faith's grandmother who lives in Manchester and is visiting for a few days, has come to see how she's doing. Faith shows her the toys. Lil tells her to put them away and join them downstairs. She leaves. Faith, absorbed, continues to lay out the train track. Then she opens another box and finds a storybook. It is German, entitled *Der Rattenfänger*. Faith senses something familiar. Is this the story that her mother used to tell her at bedtime when she was little?

Helga reads Eva's storybook to her, a version of the Pied Piper of Hamelin tale about how the children in the town are enchanted away by the haunting Ratcatcher. From the shadows in the attic, a shape stirs: the figure of the Ratcatcher himself emerges. Faith does not see him. She is immersed in the book. As the story is told, Eva puts on her coat, carries her suitcase and boards the train for England. The journey progresses apace and the German border comes nearer. Suddenly, the Ratcatcher is transformed into a Nazi Border Official. When he searches her case he finds the harmonica. He makes Eva play it. She stumbles over the notes. He seems to find this amusing and does not send her back home, but gives her a sweetie for her trouble. Eva rages at the Nazis as she crosses the border into Holland.

Helga, back in Germany, continues to read the story that warns all naughty children to beware of the Ratcatcher for he will come to take them away unless they are good.

Faith is entranced by the book.

Eva's journey takes her to the boat that sails across the English Channel to Harwich, where she disembarks and is amazed to find that here in England no one wants to search her.

Scene Two

Helga has now disappeared.

Faith is looking at some letters that she has found, along with some photos, in the storybook box. The letters are from a girl called Eva to her parents in Germany.

Eva is waiting at Euston Station for her foster mother to collect her. The Ratcatcher has now transformed himself into an Organiser who is organising the children from the Kindertransport. He tells her that her foster mother has been delayed and she'll have to wait. Eva can't speak English and wrongly understands that no one is coming to meet her. She bursts into tears. The Organiser tries to be sympathetic but is clearly thrown by having to deal with lots of needy, foreign children who only speak German. He gives her his handkerchief and disappears.

Lil, losing patience with Faith, returns to the attic. Why hasn't she put away the things that she has so messily removed from the boxes?

Eva is still waiting to be picked up. In an instant, Lil turns to her and becomes younger by more than forty-five years. She has at last arrived to take Eva home and shows her onto another train to Manchester. Eva immediately connects with Lil's warmth and down-to-earth manner. Even though neither can speak the other's language, she even persuades her new foster mother to let her have a puff of her cigarette.

Lil urges Faith to clear up now, but Faith is preoccupied with the letters and photos that she has discovered. She asks Lil why she has never mentioned the German girl that came to stay with her during the war. Lil becomes defensive. Faith persists. Lil insists that she put away her mother's things. Faith is suddenly struck by an astonishing realisation: is this little refugee girl her mother? Lil does not deny it. Faith is stunned. Why had she always been told that her mother was adopted when she was a baby?

Eva, having now been in Manchester for a couple of months, asks for Lil's help with a letter that she is writing to apply for permits for her parents to come to Britain. Lil is impressed at how well her English is developing. They agree on the wording for an advertisement to find employers who need domestic servants (the only work they are permitted to do as immigrants) and also become sponsors in order to get permits to enter Britain.

Faith asks Lil to tell her the truth about her mother. Lil hesitantly shares the basic details of Eva's background and arrival in England. She is very concerned that Evelyn must not be troubled with Faith's discovery.

Eva tries to sneak up to her room without Lil noticing her. Lil catches her and demands to know why she is home so late. Eva admits that she has been to an affluent part of Manchester where she has been knocking on doors to find someone to employ her parents. Lil is furious. She urges Eva to trust her to take care of this. Eva is afraid that Lil will send her away if she's naughty. Lil assures her that she won't send her away, not even if she is naughty.

Evelyn returns to the attic. Lil tries to play down the mess and get Faith to clear up. Faith asks Evelyn outright about Eva Schlesinger and, when Evelyn refuses to respond, confronts her mother about who she really is and why she has never told her about her background. Evelyn is stern and icy, then tries to leave. Faith loses her temper and blocks her way, demanding that she is given some answers. Evelyn remains aloof. Faith storms out of the attic, followed by a furious Lil.

Evelyn is left alone as the shadow of the Ratcatcher looms and Eva, terrified, begs to be protected from him.

Act Two

Scene One

It is night.

Evelyn, unkempt and withdrawn, sits alone in the attic smoking beside an ashtray of cigarette butts.

Helga and Eva sit together on their last evening together, after the case has been packed and the story has been read. Evelyn does not acknowledge their presence.

Tentative knocking. It is Faith. She asks Evelyn to unlock the door and let her in. Evelyn tells her to go away.

Somebody is chanting 'Sieg Heil.' Eva draws away from Helga. The Ratcatcher approaches in the guise of a Manchester Postman who is larking about, aping a German stormtrooper. He also tries to impersonate Hitler, asking Eva to teach him how to salute in the Nazi style. He doesn't understand why being Jewish makes her reluctant to do this. He thinks that all Germans love Hitler. He delivers a parcel from her family. It contains the *Rattenfänger* book and a Haggadah, the religious book that is used by Jews when celebrating the festival of Passover. In the letter that arrives with the books, Helga urges Eva to observe the festival and live a Jewish life.

More knocking on the attic door. Lil threatens to call the fire brigade if Evelyn doesn't let her in.

Evelyn unlocks the door and Lil at once advises her to talk to Faith. Evelyn can't bear to do this. She believes that Faith hates and blames her and nothing she can do can change this.

Eva is wearing her coat and carries her case and gas mask. She is standing once again on a train platform. The Second World War has just begun and she is being evacuated from Manchester to the countryside where they will be safe from German bombings of the city. Lil is concerned about her wearing the gold jewellery from her mother but Eva will not remove it. Then Eva sees a shadow. She is afraid. She asks Lil not to make her go. Lil reassures her that this is for her own safety and hurries her onto the train. As it pulls out of the station, Eva, overwhelmed with terror that the Ratcatcher will get her, opens the door and leaps off the moving train onto the platform. Lil rushes to her aid and agrees that she can remain with her in Manchester.

Evelyn asks Lil what she had best do with the papers in the box. She had kept them because, amongst the personal items, there are official documents that confirm her right to stay in the country, including those granting her British citizenship. She doesn't want Faith to see any of this. She starts to rip to pieces anything that is not 'official'. Lil offers to help. Evelyn accuses her of 'doing too much', of making her betray her mother. Lil doesn't understand what she means. Evelyn doesn't explain. Together they continue to rip each letter and photo to shreds.

Eva is waiting on another station platform for a train to arrive. She holds a photograph of her parents. The Ratcatcher appears, as a Station Guard. The last train has already arrived. He tells her to go home. Eva refuses to accept this. Her parents sent word and are coming to England and she is here to meet them. The Guard becomes suspicious when he hears her accent and accuses her of being a spy. Lil arrives and confirms that her parents can't come now because the war has started. Eva is devastated. Lil invites her to come to church to pray for them. Eva removes the jewellery. She doesn't want to wear it any longer.

Evelyn and Lil continue to tear the letters and photos.

Time has passed and the war is nearly over. Inside a cinema, Lil and Eva are watching a newsreel reporting the liberation of Belsen concentration camp. Lil at once bustles Eva, now fifteen, out of the auditorium. Lil is markedly more upset than Eva, who is self-contained and more concerned about not missing the main feature film.

Faith knocks on the attic door again. Evelyn still has some more papers to destroy. Lil tells Faith that they'll let her in soon.

Eva has something to suggest whilst Lil hems her new dress. She wants to sell the jewellery from her mother to help pay her keep. Lil insists that she keep all of it safe. Eva in turn insists that she will never wear it ever again. Now that she knows for sure that her parents are dead, she wants to leave the past behind. She will sell it.

Evelyn tears the final photo. Now she is finished. Lil lets Faith into the attic. Faith is horrified at what her mother has done. How will she ever find out about her family now? Evelyn agrees to tell her what she can remember if Faith promises not to ask her about it again. Faith agrees. Evelyn tells her what little she recalls. Faith asks what happened to her parents. Evelyn says that her father died in a concentration camp. Faith asks about her mother.

The attic falls silent.

Evelyn says simply that Helga did not die.

Helga appears, utterly transformed, a living spectre.

Evelyn, Faith and Lil all watch as Eva, now seventeen, approaches. Helga has survived the war and is meeting Eva in Liverpool, where she intends to take a boat to New York where her brother is now living and where she and Eva will make a new life together. She is shocked to hear that Eva has now changed her name to Evelyn and been adopted by Lil and her husband.

Scene Two

The attic is has been tidied.

Helga waits beside her suitcase.

Evelyn is once again looking through the boxes for household items to give to Faith, who is preparing to leave home and move in with her friends. This time she clearly means to go. They are nearly done. Faith takes a box downstairs.

Lil pops in to say that she's going out for the afternoon. Evelyn offers to take her to the station tomorrow to catch her train home to Manchester. Their exchange is slightly tense. Lil clearly had not been aware that Evelyn's mother, Helga, had survived. Lil agrees to let Evelyn take her to the station. As Lil leaves, Faith arrives to collect the next box and Evelyn offers her more cutlery and crockery. Faith wants to know if she is Jewish and asks Evelyn about being German. Evelyn plays down the Jewishness and affirms how important being baptised and becoming Christian then being granted a British passport was to her. She does, however, give Faith a few remaining objects from her childhood: a harmonica, the *Rattenfänger* book and the Haggadah. Faith takes the last box downstairs.

On a Liverpool quayside, Eva, now young Evelyn, joins Helga, who is about to board ship to take her to New York. She urges her daughter to join her and cannot understand why she is so distant when they are fortunate enough to have been given the opportunity to be reunited when so many others have died. All Evelyn can do is wish Helga a safe trip. They part. As Helga turns to go, Evelyn finds herself speaking directly to her, revealing that it was she, her own mother, who was transformed in her eyes into the Ratcatcher who threatened to take her away from the place that had become her home. Helga expresses her own suffering, accuses and blames. Evelyn cracks open and says what the little girl that last night in Hamburg felt deep down: she wished only to stay with her parents, even if that meant death, rather than be sent away. But she was made to go and she had to find a way to survive on her own. Helga leaves.

Faith returns to the attic to find her mother crying. She encourages her to share her feelings with her. Evelyn cannot do this. Faith asks for her box of toys. Evelyn gives them to her. Faith leaves.

Evelyn remains alone in the attic. The shadow of the Ratcatcher lingers.

Nigel Hastings as the Ratcatcher in his guise as the Border Official and Julia Malewski as Eva in the 1996 Watford Palace Theatre production © Donald Cooper/Photostage

Time, Space and Theatre

'The only reason for time is so that everything doesn't happen at once.' *Albert Einstein*

'I personally would like to bring a tortoise on the stage, turn it into a racehorse, then into a hat, a song, a dragoon and a fountain of water. One can dare anything in the theatre.' *Eugène Ionesco*

The playscript of *Kindertransport* is like a map.

Just as a map is a two-dimensional representation of a three-dimensional place, so the script is a plan for a live theatre production. Consider the difference between looking at the contour lines on a piece of paper that describe a hill and actually walking up a hill. This is similar to the contrast between reading a scene on the page then performing or watching it on stage. To understand *Kindertransport* fully the play needs to be 'put on its feet' and enacted. Read the script with this in mind – in fact, try to move it in space if at all possible – and it will communicate so much more clearly on so many more levels.

> Dear Ms Samuels,
>
> I am currently studying English literature and we have been studying your play *Kindertransport*. I love the way you have the past and present on either side of the stage and I would like to know how you came across the idea and also why didn't you just have the past and present at different intervals?

Students of the text often refer to 'split staging'. They also ask about 'flashbacks'. On first encountering the script, it might seem that the stage is split into a 'past' section and a 'present' section. Eva's story can also be seen as something that happened a long time before the Evelyn story. However, this way of approaching the play is simply a first step towards understanding how it really works.

Just as *Kindertransport* is set in a single place, Evelyn's attic, that contains many places, so it also occurs in a single time – the present – that includes many times.

Greek philosophers identified two different types of time.

'Chronos' time is clock time, measured in seconds, minutes, hours, days, weeks, years, centuries, millennia, etc. This is perceived as a linear continuum. In 'chronos' time we have a sense of past, present and future. It is, if you like, horizontal with a before and after.

'Kairos' time is measured, if it can be measured, or rather encountered, in moments. In 'kairos' time everything is always happening at once and there is no distinction between past, present and future. Everything occurs in one time only: now. This is vertical time with no before and no after, because all is simultaneous.

Kindertransport may seem to be occurring in a chronological time frame, and there is a sense of this in the play, but it is primarily operating in a 'kairos' zone.

This 'Now' in the attic, this attic in the 'Now', exists on two levels of reality: literal and metaphorical.

'Literal' reality is the physical, actual dimension that can be seen, touched, heard, smelt with the senses. As I write this, I am sitting at my desk in the basement of my home in North London. I can smell the remains of the coffee that coats the bottom of the mug that stands beside my computer screen. I can hear a dog barking in the distance. All this belongs to literal reality.

'Metaphorical' reality is that which is invisible, untouchable, poetic and represents something more essential and abstract. As I write this, I am also digging for answers to the questions that call to me about the roots of this play. Now, I do not literally have a spade in my hand and I am not actually digging a hole in my basement floor. I cannot literally hear the sound of a question, nor does this question have an actual mouth with which to call. The play does not have physical roots like the abundant sage that is sprouting just outside the window. I am describing here my inner state that exists in the realm of emotion, imagination, symbol, consciousness and understanding.

On a literal level, the attic in which *Kindertransport* is set is physically made of wood and brick, has floorboards, possibly has a skylight and a door through which people can enter and leave, and it is at the top of Evelyn's house, just beneath the roof.

On a metaphorical level, this attic also represents Evelyn's 'psyche'. This is the word from which 'psychology', 'psychiatrists', 'psychotic', etc., are derived. It originates in Greek and means 'soul'.

The attic is not only a physical space in her home that Evelyn can inhabit, it is also an emotional space that represents what is going on inside her. So, at the very start of the play when the attic contains Eva and Helga, this is how the audience first encounters Evelyn, for Helga and Eva are not separate from but a part of Evelyn. In *Kindertransport*, the central character is introduced 'from the inside out'. We see what is going on invisibly within Evelyn before the physical character presents herself, and we see her in the flesh from the outside. Normally we meet people from 'the outside in'. From the first moment, the play declares itself as a piece that invites its audience into the interior of its central character. It is a deeply psychological play.

There is also yet another level of reality on which the play operates. This is the 'mythical' level, which links to the 'metaphorical'. There is one character particularly who embodies this dimension – the Ratcatcher. He connects with something greater than Evelyn's personal psyche, tapping into the universal human condition. Psychoanalyst Carl Jung identified this shared state of being as 'the collective unconscious'. In this realm we meet 'archetypes' that symbolise specific themes or qualities that connect all humans on the blueprint level of our make-up psychologically and, some might say, spiritually. So, this attic is a mythical space too in which the great sweep and depth of human experience is invoked.

The poet William Blake wrote:

> To see a World in a Grain of Sand,
> And a Heaven in a Wild Flower,
> Hold Infinity in the palm of your hand
> And Eternity in an hour.

When children play, they naturally enter 'kairos' time and use whatever is to hand to bring alive an imagined world that feels just as real as the physical reality that they also inhabit. Play is the medium through which the inner finds a place in the outer life, and vice versa. So a chair can represent and also be treated and physically experienced as a throne or a tree or a portal to Mars or a dog or a wigwam or a well or a cage or anything a child likes. Theatre is essentially about playing. Within Evelyn's attic, every one of the literal objects can also become anything: an old wardrobe might change from a train carriage to a Manchester house to a cinema in a split second.

The beauty of theatre is that it is by its very nature a conscious embodiment of all these levels of reality at once. As a live art form, audience and actors gather together in the same actual place where they can see, hear, smell, touch and feel what is going on in this shared environment. Theatre is a physical experience for all concerned. There is also a collective agreement to create a metaphorical space within the physical framework. As a group, audience and actors 'suspend disbelief' in order to 'make believe' together that something is happening that is not literally happening. None of the actors are literally the characters they are playing. They are pretending. Sometimes the play might appear to copy actual life experience and take on a 'naturalistic' form, sometimes it might be utterly fantastical and bear no relation to physical reality. Most importantly of all, theatre takes everyone involved, when it is set up with care and when it works, into a shared experience of 'kairos' time and enables all to access the quintessential moment when all levels of reality merge and come together, and the inner and outer selves of individuals and the collective merge as one.

In *Kindertransport*, then, present time includes past and future, so there is no separation to either side of the stage and the characters, and action from different eras move around each other, sometimes in very close proximity, like a tapestry being woven before your eyes. Everything is interconnected. Life works on many levels and through many layers. The play expresses, if you like, a multidimensional view of many realities that all occur at once.

This is not a naturalistic play. It is expressionistic. Imagination is needed to bring it to life.

It is also a 'feminine' play in the sense that it is deeply intimate and inhabits the private world. Traditionally, theatre is the realm of the 'masculine' and the public domain of action and interaction out in the world. One of my aims with this play is to enable people to gather together in a communal experience to share feelings that are usually kept very private, to touch something alongside each other that often we do not even dare to touch within ourselves on our own. Most of all, *Kindertransport* is a play written from the heart, calling to the heart. In opening our hearts together and probing the invisible parts of our psyches, personal and collective, we can experience imaginatively what we fear, what hurts and what we yearn to be healed.

Early Drafts

'The dead are alive; the living are their ghosts.' *Note on the cover of the second draft of* Kindertransport, *1992*

'My first draft usually only has a few elements worth keeping. I have to find out what those are and build from them and throw out what doesn't work, or what simply is not alive.'
Susan Sontag

'I start drawing, and eventually the characters involve themselves in a situation. Then in the end, I go back and try to cut out most of the preachments.' *Dr Seuss*

During the development of the first draft of *Kindertransport*, I attended a workshop run by Mark Ravenhill. In those days, Mark was yet to become established as a playwright and I knew him as a workshop leader and theatre director through the Soho Theatre Company, whose remit was to develop and produce original plays by new writers. I had written the first act of Evelyn and Eva's story and was still exploring how the piece might be shaped. Much of my teens in Liverpool had been spent involved in youth theatre where we devised our own plays as pieces of 'ensemble' theatre. Inspired by this approach, I had directed a number of group-developed theatre pieces at university and then went on to become a drama teacher in inner-London secondary schools. So, the opportunity to explore the scriptwriting of this new play using practical methods was very welcome and familiar. I was beginning to discover then that writing a play takes many drafts, much rewriting, sometimes a shattering of what has been developed and a radical reworking, to discover the form needed to enable the piece to become its fully realised self.

Mark had read what had been written so far and asked me to take the 'hot seat' as Evelyn. There is a world of difference between writing in a character's voice and physically inhabiting his or her skin. As I sat on the chair in front of the group of emerging playwrights, I knew immediately that Evelyn found herself in what felt like a storage room. As the questions came, this room, this world, this woman took shape. I sensed what Evelyn was sensing, the dimness, the orderliness of the stashed boxes, a lot of boxes. Then I realised that there was a box on the floor not far from where I was sitting. I was asked what was inside this box. As Evelyn, I clammed up. I wasn't interested in this box. It didn't matter. The other writers and Mark pressed me to give my attention to it. The more they persisted, the more stubborn I became. Then Evelyn was invited to pick up this imaginary but all-too-real box. I simply could not touch it. My body as her body recoiled. After encouragement, I did pick it up and looked inside but was utterly unable to remove a single item. I was asked to describe what it contained. I managed to say that there were photos and 'things like that'. I was asked to take out a photo and share it. I utterly refused. When pressed again, I burst into tears. When I left the hot seat and emerged from the role, we discussed what I had experienced and what the rest of the group had witnessed from their perspective. This 'role-play' exercise was invaluable and gave me real, actual insight into the state of Evelyn's denial, strength of character and emotional fragility. It enabled me to continue work on the script and complete a first draft.

In this very first draft of the play, the scene continued to be set in a 'storage room'. It was Abigail Morris, director of the first production of the play in 1993 for Soho Theatre Company at the Cockpit Theatre, who suggested the more evocative attic setting. Still, a relic of this first version remains in the published script today which is still introduced as being set in a 'dusty storage room'. Also in the first draft, Evelyn's daughter is named Hope. This was changed to Faith in subsequent drafts because a woman called Hope, one of

whose parents had been on the Kindertransport, helped me
with research and it seemed wise to avoid implicating her in
any way in the story. It is always important to sense when to
distance actual life experience from the fiction so that the two
are distinct.

KINDERTRANSPORT –
FIRST DRAFT, CIRCA 1990/91
Act One, Scene One

*A 'spare' storage room. Junk, cases, tea chests and boxes lying
around.*

*From somewhere deep below the pile of stuff, deep within one of
the boxes, emanate the faint strains of a simple tune being
played on a mouth organ.*

The door opens.

HOPE *stands in the doorway. She looks at the boxes, gets the
measure of them. She opens some of the top boxes and looks
into them. She finds hats, plastic cutlery, Christmas
decorations. She moves the top boxes to get beneath. She
opens some more boxes. She finds an old train set. She takes
out the trains, control box, model platforms, people and
signals. She lays them lovingly on the floor, making a
station.*

HOPE (*holding her nose*). The train soon to be arriving at
platform two…

*She turns back to the boxes and starts to open them quickly.
She looks and rummages around in each one. She takes out
a carefully wrapped and preserved girl's party dress in the
style of the early seventies.*

'When I was five I was barely alive.'

She wraps up the dress again.

*The mouth-organ music gets louder as the boxes on top are
removed.*

Suddenly HOPE*'s ear catches the melody of the mouth
organ. She is drawn towards it as if by magic.*

She moves boxes and bags, giving them a cursory looking at.

Finally she reaches the box from which the music is coming. By it is a battered old suitcase with a leather belt around it. She picks up the suitcase.

My God. Oh, my God. She did keep… she did…

She tries to open the case. It is locked. She reaches to open the large box containing the music.

EVELYN *stands in the doorway.*

EVELYN. What are you doing?

The music stops.

HOPE (*withdrawing quickly from the box*). I thought you were…

EVELYN. This is my room.

HOPE. My things are in here…

EVELYN. What things?

HOPE. From when I was a kid.

EVELYN. Tell me what you want and I'll get it for you.

HOPE. I don't know exactly…

EVELYN. Don't know?

HOPE. I just wanted to look. To see what there was. I can't remember everything.

EVELYN. I know what's in here. Ask me.

HOPE. Where are my dolls?

EVELYN (*surveying the disarrayed boxes, etc.*). I can't tell. You've moved everything.

HOPE. Will you help me search for them?

EVELYN. What? Now?

HOPE. I'd like to find them.

EVELYN. I've only just got in…

HOPE. Please.

EVELYN *stands very still and quiet.*

HOPE. What's the matter?

EVELYN. Come out of here.

HOPE. Mother.

EVELYN. Just come on out.

HOPE. What about my dolls?

EVELYN. Another time.

HOPE. If you don't want to search, I'll just do it on my
    own...

EVELYN. I'll find them for you when I have a moment.

HOPE. Are you telling me that I'm not allowed in this room?

EVELYN. I'm asking you, Hope...

HOPE. Asking me what?

EVELYN. Not to poke around.

HOPE. I'm not poking around!

EVELYN. You... are.

    Pause.

HOPE. I'm sorry.

EVELYN. You've been saying that a lot lately.

HOPE. I don't want to upset you. I just...

EVELYN. I've got some teacakes. Shall we go down for tea?

    The mouth-organ music starts again. HOPE *hears it and is
    transfixed. She looks in the direction of the box.*

They're Marks and Spencer teacakes.

HOPE. I'm not hungry.

    EVELYN *looks at the box.*

    She takes HOPE *by the hand.*

EVELYN. Let's go.

    EVELYN *leads* HOPE *out.*

    *The music becomes louder and louder until it fills the entire
    room.*

In this early version, the first character we meet is Evelyn's daughter. We see her discover something that her mother has hidden and yet, when Evelyn finds her there, she does not come clean about this or raise it with her mother. She also knows what has happened to Evelyn but is clearly not allowed to mention it.

In the next scene, Evelyn locks herself in the room and, as soon as she turns the key, Helga and Eva spring to life on the night before Eva is sent away. Then the journey and the Rat-catcher story are told in parallel. Evelyn is the one directly experiencing this reliving of her earlier life, rather than Faith discovering it and not knowing what it is or means at first. So, the structure for the first draft is that, more or less from the outset, Evelyn locks herself into the storage room and Hope is trying to get her to open the door and talk to her. It is Hope who phones Lily Music (the earlier name for Lil) and asks her to come over to help persuade Evelyn to emerge. Inside the room, Evelyn is overwhelmed by a re-experiencing of Eva's journey.

A little later in the Act One of this version, it is not the Postman (in Act Two in the revised and current version) but Helga's brother, Onkel Klaus, who visits Eva about six months before the war begins, on his way to New York. Klaus had been arrested then released from a Nazi prison camp and has managed to escape from Germany. Helga has given him the package containing the Ratcatcher book and a letter to give to Eva.

KINDERTRANSPORT — FIRST DRAFT, CIRCA 1990/91
Act One, Scene Four

LILY *exits, closing the door behind her.*

EVELYN *watches her go, thinks to herself, then settles down to reading and tearing up some more papers.*

Sounds of a quayside. A boat is about to leave. It is busy, lots of people, noise, activity.

KLAUS. Eva!

EVA. Onkel Klaus?

KLAUS. You've grown. So like your mother...

EVA. Is it really you, Onkel Klaus? Is it?

KLAUS. It is me. Yes, I am not an apparition. I am indeed here. In Liverpool. In England.

EVA. You're...

KLAUS. ...different?

EVA. Yes.

KLAUS. Thinner?

EVA. Your hair.

KLAUS. I thought I could do with a change. Here, feel it.

EVA *hesitates.*

Go on.

EVA *tentatively strokes his shaved head.*

It's all the rage, you know. New German style. Everyone's got it.

EVA (*panicking*). Even Mutti and Vati?

KLAUS. No. No. They wanted to keep their hair as it was. They look just the same as always.

KLAUS *checks his watch.*

We haven't got long. Boats don't wait for people. They go when they want to. If I hadn't had to spend so much time in London, I could have seen more of you. Could have come to Manchester. This is so rushed. Silly to be so rushed. What a shame. Terrible. Still...

EVA. Did they give you anything?

KLAUS. Who?

EVA. Mutti and Vati?

KLAUS. Oh yes. Yes. Of course. They wanted to send a case, but – (*Gives her a bag.*) this was all I could manage.

EVA. Thank you.

KLAUS. Better than nothing.

She opens the bag and takes out the storybook and a letter. She just holds them awkwardly.

EVA. How are they?

KLAUS. They're well. Talking a lot about you and your lovely English family. Looking forward to meeting them.

EVA. We got them jobs and the permits are going through. Mrs Music helped me.

KLAUS. You're a clever girl, saving your family like this. A real heroine.

EVA. We're the lucky ones, aren't we?

KLAUS. Yes we are. Very lucky.

EVA. Maybe we can come to America to visit you one day.

KLAUS. You better had. Clara and Tantchen Anna are loving it out there. Tantchen Anna says that Clara has an American accent even.

EVA. I know English. It's not so hard to learn.

KLAUS. It's easier for children than for adults. I'll take a bit longer I should think. What about this… (*Stiffly and with a strong German accent.*) 'Hello, Miss Schlesinger. I am very pleased to make your acquaintance.'

EVA. Welcome to England, Mr Grunstein.

KLAUS. A good start then.

EVA. Was it horrid at the prison camp?

KLAUS. Who told you?

EVA. I heard Tantchen Anna telling Mutti.

KLAUS. That you should have to know such things.

EVA. They didn't think they'd let you out.

KLAUS. You never know what they'll do. One minute this, the next minute that. Fill a hole here. Dig it out again. Put in water. Empty out the water. Shovel in sand. Shovel it out again. Pile up stones. Unpile the stones. Clean the paving stones…

EVA. Dirty the paving stones.

They both laugh then stop and realise.

KLAUS. I shouldn't tell you. I signed a paper not to tell.

EVA. I won't say to anyone.

KLAUS. Good girl.

> KLAUS *looks at his watch.*

> The boat will go. My time has come. Such a short meeting. Still, at least I saw you. I'll write and tell your parents. I'll have lots of time to write now. When they come they won't recognise you.

This draft was subjected to detailed feedback and notes from Abigail Morris and the then Literary Manager at the Soho Theatre Company, Jack Bradley. They suggested that having Klaus visit Eva and so raise a strong image of a labour camp this early in the action undermined the power of the crucial moment much later in the play when Eva/Evelyn faces what has happened to her parents in the Holocaust. I was encouraged to cut Onkel Klaus. So in the next draft the handing over of the package from home was allotted to the Postman who refers to the Nazi regime in Germany through the ill-informed eyes of an Englishman. Still, losing Onkel Klaus left a gap. The spectral presence of the camp survivor belonged somehow in the play. In this first draft, both Eva's parents are killed during the Holocaust. It wasn't until a number of drafts later, after a great deal of rewriting through various stages, that I was up late one night working on the rehearsal draft for the production. I was tired and addressing some notes in the scene towards the end of Act Two, Scene One in which Faith asks Evelyn to tell her whatever she can remember and then asks what happened to her parents. Evelyn replies that they died. Faith presses her and she says that her father died in 1943 in Auschwitz. Faith asks what has happened to her mother. Suddenly, as I was rewriting the scene, Helga walked onto the page and made her presence felt. She made it clear that she had not died. This was as much of a surprise to me that night as it is now when an audience or reader first encounter it. In the Onkel Klaus scene are the small seeds that will later grow into this climactic and revelatory moment. I could not have thought up or planned this mentally. The inspiration for this play comes as much from my own unconscious as it is an exploration of Evelyn's.

Eva

'Create living people; people not characters.' *Ernest Hemingway*

'Mrs Roberts said; "We give you a home, and you must keep it nice," and I thought; and if we don't keep it nice you won't give us a home?' *From Inge's Diary in* We Came As Children: A Collective Autobiography of Refugees, *ed. Karen Gershon*

Eva was the name of my ex-husband's aunt who grew up initially in Hamburg, Germany, and fled with her family to Palestine in 1933 soon after Hitler came to power. I met her when she was around sixty and living in the outskirts of Tel Aviv in Israel. She showed me photographs of her early years in Germany. One photo in particular showed her class at elementary school before she left. Every child in the regimented rows, wearing their neatly turned-out uniforms, was blonde and Eva alone stood out with her dark hair. I named the character after her partly because of this image highlighting her experience of belonging and not belonging to a group, being so very different in the midst of another world. The sight of it made her partly smile, partly grimace over fifty years later. Her experience contrasted markedly from the character's because this Eva was not separated from her family. She travelled with them to live the rest of her life in what was to become a Jewish state.

The age of nine seems to be a crucial, cusp age. In cases where a 'Kind' was older than nine when sent away, he or she was more likely to be able to reconnect with a surviving parent if they were reunited. If younger, then they were less likely to be able to do this. Those of nine and under have also tended to lose all trace of a German accent whereas those older often still retain their German accent. Eva is at the top end of the younger age group. I wanted her to be a bit independent, to be able to go out and knock on doors like she does, but still need mothering.

Sarah Shanson was twelve years old when she auditioned to play the role of Eva in the first production of *Kindertransport* produced by Soho Theatre Company at the Cockpit Theatre in 1993. During rehearsals she celebrated her thirteenth birthday. She has since worked as an actor, singer, musician and composer for the Royal Opera House, Young Vic, Royal Philharmonic Orchestra, National Theatre, BBC and many others. She has also worked on arts educational projects for several organisations, including the Orchestra of the Age of Enlightenment and the Guildhall School of Music & Drama. She was involved in setting up the Anchor Project, a charity for unaccompanied refugee children in Brixton, and worked for JCORE (The Jewish Council for Racial Equality) with unaccompanied asylum-seeking children. She was nominated for Best Actress in the London Fringe Awards for her performance as Eva.

I met Sarah and discussed Eva again with her twenty years after the play's premiere, in summer 2013, when she was in her early thirties and now had two children of her own. I was immediately struck by how her own life experience and struggles with a sense of Jewishness and 'belonging' chimed with some of the questions that Eva herself has to face.

> I lived in North London, not far from Golders Green, and went to the Finchley Children's Music Group. The lady there started sending some of the kids to auditions. Anyway, she sent me along to an audition because I think the brief was a certain height, a certain colour hair, Jewish... or someone who looked that way, which is interesting because I perceived myself as Jewish but didn't ever perceive myself as looking anything in particular. I was hugely influenced by Jewish culture and recent historical experience, but my mum isn't Jewish... well, she converted to Reform Judaism before I was born. My dad is Jewish. There was always a sort of underlying rejection from mainstream institutions and some individuals, and a few distant members of my dad's family as well. There were lots of social events around

different youth groups and synagogues and I always felt like I had something to hide.

I remember once going to 'cheder' [Jewish 'Sunday school'] and I mentioned to another child that my mum wasn't Jewish, because I didn't understand the matrilineal thing at that point because I was so little [Jewishness is, by tradition, inherited directly through the mother – so if a mother is Jewish then that automatically makes the child Jewish]. And the other kid went, 'Aaaah!' and ran around and told everyone, and told the teacher. The teacher then left the room to find the Rabbi to ask him what I was doing there. I just remember very intensely feeling like I wanted the ground to swallow me whole. Even in the Reform movement there was a feeling that it's a race thing, not a religion thing. So it was just quite confusing because I've got this surname and I'm being told that I look it and yet I'm not it. I think that probably did affect my understanding of the role, but in an instinctive way because I don't think I processed it in any way, shape or form.

I'd go to synagogue on Rosh Hashana and Yom Kippur [Jewish New Year and Day of Atonement, major festivals in the Jewish calendar] and we didn't eat pork in the house. There were certain attitudes that prevailed: very close family, bonds with your parents, duty. I identified myself as Jewish because I grew up in that area. It was the thing about me that was noticed more than the other side of my background. My mum's family are cattle farmers in Wales. It was very different cultural experiences when we'd go to Wales. They're very loving, very accepting. They would also take the piss out of us because we were English. Then they'd say, 'But you're not English, you're Hebrew.' It's like, being identified by different people, other people telling you what you are. And I was like, 'But I don't know what I am.' It's just confusing. You're told that you are something, or you're not something.

Drawing on her own experience of Jewishness and identity was crucial in enabling her to find the character of Eva from within rather than putting on a display of how she might appear. Sarah was learning about what acting truly requires.

At my audition I was asked to pretend to be nine years old and my parents had left and I couldn't find them anywhere. I remember sitting on the floor rocking at one point. I think I definitely overdid it. I don't think I would react in that way. But I thought, 'This is my opportunity to show how much pain I possess.'

When I saw the script for the first time I think I found it so big and so many time shifts that I found it quite overwhelming. I couldn't envisage it. I'd never really done anything like that before. I remember the readthrough and meeting the other members of the cast, just feeling quite scared. Of course the script changed so much in the process of rehearsals. It's quite a mystical process, really, from the first day of rehearsals to performance, how much it changed. It became a flowing emotional journey, whereas in that first instance, well I was only twelve in that first reading, I was coming at it trying to get my head around what was literally going on all the time. The clarity of how Abigail directed it made it all link in the way that it should, or if it did appear to be disjointed it was right – it had a clear through-purpose. Once I'd learned the lines it was all so much easier because you're away from the page and you're there with other people in the moment.

Even though she had played the role more than half her lifetime before, Sarah still retained a strong sense of Eva's development through the play from dependent child to independent young adult.

At the beginning I used to feel so sorry for Eva because she's so young. To be forced to make such a long journey on your own at that age is just fundamentally wrong, isn't it? I think as well at the time, nine years old wasn't so long ago. Even when I was thirteen, it was only four years before and I could recollect how horrifying just the thought is of being left alone in the big, wide world, abandoned by your parents... They didn't want to abandon her... but the sort of sickening sense of being pushed away by a parent whom you love and need, that was very tangible. And yeah, regardless of the reason, that feels like rejection.

In playing Eva, the physical and emotional reality of this child's viewpoint needs to be fully embodied.

> I remember delivering it quite straight, quite innocently, or at least feeling that that was how I was doing it, like a child does. A thought pops into your head and you just say it, and you just do it. Yes a child's going to have moments of realising it themselves and being frightened, but they're also very 'in the moment' and she sings her little song, she does her childish things and carries on and carries through it because I suppose that is the one blessing of being a child, you're not always aware of the larger context of what's happening. It can be terrifying. It can also be helpful in certain circumstances.

In her very different relationships with Helga, her birth mother, and foster mother, Lil, Eva also encounters contrasting aspects of mothering.

> Helga is formal, because she's quite Germanic. But at the same time it's not formal out of coldness but out of cultural norms. It's like, 'We are proper people, we have nice clothes, we behave in a socially acceptable way because we've got certain standards to uphold and we are trying our best to be a 'mensch' [Yiddish for a decent, good person], and that's not actually cold, it's a manner of being, and in that relationship there's obviously an incredible amount of love. The sacrifice the mother made was the hugest sacrifice you can give.

> I remember Lil more as a sort of presence, very warm, steady, accepting, a bit brusque, in that very British way: 'Don't fuss, don't cry. I'm here, I'm strong, I'm with you, but chin up, have a cup of tea, let's do something, go for a walk in the park and you'll feel better, I don't want to talk about it,' sort of thing. She's the best thing that could have happened to Eva in many ways because dwelling on the reality of the situation, how is that going to help, particularly in that era? Now she'd be assessed as needing an incredible amount of psychological support, counselling sessions. She'd be acknowledged as having serious trauma, whereas in that era there would be no such support or recognition. So she has to adapt to that. You have to carry on.

Obviously Eva wants to be accepted by the place where her new mother comes from and wants to be like them and part of it. She tries to change. In that scene where she's fifteen, I was encouraged to do a slightly northern accent. And I was, 'Oh no, I don't think I can do that.' It was meant to be a sign that that's the kind of English she would have heard so she would have picked up the accent. And also, 'You talk like us, you are like us.' I think she would very much want to be able to erase everything. It would be so much simpler if it never happened. It's a difficult one, adoptive parent/child relationships, resentment on both sides to a certain extent, I would imagine. There's an instinct to want to belong to each other in a family and a knowledge between you that you don't really, and anger that this can't be what I want it to be even though we pretend.

Eva's fear of not belonging, of being abandoned, unprotected and threatened, finds tangible form, again from her fearful child's-eye view, in the figure of the Ratcatcher.

With the Ratcatcher, the metaphor may be for the force of illogical, malevolent scapegoating and hunting of an innocent who's the personification of that in a very childish, symbolic way from a child's story. Sadistic and completely unwarranted cruelty. He's the unsaid force that is Nazism. You're aware of the conspiracy theories against Jews. From Eva's experience as a Jew in Germany, the huge impact that's had, so other people from the wider community at large do represent danger, even if they do seem very banal, like the Postman. Sometimes whether they are dangerous or not, or whether it's just a misunderstanding, it all feeds into this larger picture of believing: 'My life is cheap to you.' So even people who would be perceived as not having much power can potentially have a lot of malignant power, and that's how I felt about the roles played by the same character as the Ratcatcher. There is an element of mystery and unpredictability about him. He is a fairytale character. That actually makes him feel more scary because he is unpredictable. He can't be defined.

My parents were both born during the war years – they had me a bit later in the day than most of their generation – so they'd seen the last bits of war and had seen the impact themselves, and I think they felt very strongly, particularly projected from my dad who was the officially Jewish one, this very profound sense that things could change and violent danger or death or something horrible, even though it sounds illogical, is a possibility at any given moment and there is something to be afraid of.

My grandmother would do the very typical thing, saying, 'everything was wonderful', and then she'd talk and talk and talk, like about being in boarding school in Germany and the other girls saying, 'Ah, the Jew smells.' And make her sleep in winter with wide-open windows. There was a very fearless teacher, and when they did a parade or show at school they were meant to shove out the most Aryan-looking child. He intentionally picked my grandma, because she was blonde, blue-eyed, and when he shoved her forward, she was pushed back by other teachers and children. He lost his job. I think he was trying to make the point 'there's no difference here'. She'd obviously been quite well-to-do, things had been okay, then she'd give examples of the children being cruel, and in the end that manifested itself in both her parents being murdered, they died in Auschwitz. It's that attitude that seems in certain contexts quite stupid and something you can get over, but taken to its full extent it's incredibly horrifying and it's real. So that seeming innocence of some of the manifestations of the Ratcatcher's character, his sort of un-knowing, his ignorance of the damage he's doing while he's doing it, and then that is underlined by the Ratcatcher himself who knows everything, who does know, is fully aware of the whole thing.

When Eva emerges as a teenager in the middle of Act Two, something deep has shifted within her and she is well on her way to transforming herself into Evelyn.

I do remember having an easier experience, feeling less embarrassed playing the nine-year-old. I felt very awkward playing the fifteen-year-old because she was actually the nearest one to my real age. In my mind, by the time she reaches seventeen she's grown up, so there's enough distance, I'm an adult and I had the costume as well, the dress and high heels, and I felt like I'm playing this role and

I understand the conflict, whereas I suppose with the scene with the fifteen-year-old there's quite a lot of shock involved [seeing the newsreel film about the liberation of the concentration camp]. I'd never really experienced that kind of shock, realising that this is what happened to my family. To play it was hard because with everything else I had some personal sense of, 'Well, I understand this. I instinctively get what the character might be feeling.' But the fifteen-year-old having such a momentous life experience, I felt a little bit worried about it.

Often, readers and audience members struggle to appreciate how Eva can turn her back on Helga when she comes to find her after the war. Standing in Eva's shoes as a young woman, it is fascinating how readily a barely teenage actress tapped into the character's powerful feelings of rejection towards her birth mother.

In a strange way, in Act Two, Scene One, where Eva/Evelyn says who she is and rejects her mother, it's a tiny flavour of, say, someone who's dumped you, and they come back and say, 'I was wrong, I want you back.' And you say, 'Well, I don't want you any more. You dumped me, who do you think you are?' Eva has a feeling of, 'Well, hold on, I'm still quite young and I'm trying to establish a sense of myself, and here you are messing it all up again.' Obviously there's heartbreak as well. Incredible conflict: this is your mum but when you were vulnerable and needed her, she was not there, and now you're not so vulnerable and your mother's trying to take you back to being a baby again, for her, so she can feel better. Eva can't bear to re-experience such disturbing, distressing emotions ever again. 'So, sorry, I can't connect with you.' This is how I interpreted it. Maybe something to do with the coldness of Helga… the attempt at being upright, and I suppose this feeling that, 'If you're so upright and so perfect and you're doing all the right things, how could you inflict this horrendous injury to my inner being that I have to live with for ever? How could you be all these things that you say you are? I feel you're a hypocrite and a liar and I don't trust you. I feel you're manipulating me and you're not acknowledging what I've been through.'

When Eva tries to explain to her, Helga's like, 'How dare you?' Even though, of course, she's too traumatised herself to hear it and needs lots of help, which I'm sure a character like her would never have got, from Eva's perspective, her mother is looking at her as an extension of herself and as part of her own projected world and what she needs her to be, rather than looking at Eva as a real person. Eva senses that and realises that's not fair.

In the final scene on the dockside, there's a fear of lack of control. There's a testing of lots of unknown boundaries. Eva has to take away her mother's power over her in order to carry on. It's unfortunate that it's a 'me or you' situation, which it is. I don't know how she could do anything any other way really. Her mum is never going to enable her to flourish in any sense. Her mum is going to devour her if she goes with her. She'll consume her with her own grief. And even though, of course, this is her mum, and she wants to comfort her and all that, she's doing all she can in her own life not to fall apart, to keep it together, then somebody else close really is falling apart and she needs her help and 'Aaagh, I'm afraid it's catching.' So that's how I felt about it. 'Yes, of course I would if I could, but I can't and I can't explain to you why I can't because you don't want to know. So if I do what you want me to do, you're going to destroy me.' So I felt that this was her reasoning.

Helga is a threat to the existence of the person Eva's trying to be, the one that is saving her and has kept her going – there's a line in the play, 'You threw me into the sea with all your baggage on my shoulders and I had to let go to float.' The reason she hasn't drowned is because she's invented this other personality and identity for herself, and her mother is threatening that. So it feels quite a visceral reason to not be able to go with her to America. It must be incredibly frightening to let that person you've become go and again be this abandoned child. I'm sure as well that the characters would not have that kind of analytical approach to anything, and I'm sure the emotions would be completely overwhelming and even if there were any other ways, any other rational course of action just wouldn't occur. No one's going to discuss their feelings.

It is this act of rejection, kept deeply secret from the moment it happens, that forms the final, key factor in Eva's transformation into Evelyn.

> Eva is left with terrible guilt. It's a shame that there is no middle ground in these situations. If only it could have been possible for Eva to keep her life as it is, and also maintain contact with her mother, slowly build a relationship with her again and come to some kind of peace, even give each other some comfort in later life.

> A lot of Evelyn's motivations are out of self-preservation. Eva develops those motivations over time and her behavior slowly transforms into Evelyn's. I don't think she [Evelyn] is formed, I think she's created. I think over the following decades Evelyn develops into the character you see as Faith's mother, and she must have been affected by her divorce and being the parent of a child, all those things. So by the end of the play the elements that I acted lead to Evelyn being born.

> Eva starts off incredibly vulnerable. As Eva, you realise how bloody awful it is to be vulnerable. You try to change. It's such an effort to change, so that you don't have to be that any more, that you empower yourself and you make the best out of the life you've been given and unfortunately, as much as you try, those things will remain. I suppose, very simply, that's it.

Diana Quick as Evelyn and Julia Malewski as Eva in the 1996 Watford Palace Theatre production © Donald Cooper/Photostage

Evelyn

'I'm not sure whether it's a symptom of coming from a Germanic
background or being traumatised that she is very ordered and
slightly prickly as an adult – could be either, could be both.'
Sarah Shanson (actress playing Eva) on Evelyn

'If you dig deep enough, all our secrets are the same… deep
down below there is the hard rock of the common denominator,
the sameness of our secrets.' *Amos Oz, speaking on BBC Two's*
Start the Week, *25th February 2001*

My mother came to see *Kindertransport* during its first run.
She turned to me afterwards and asked what had inspired me
to create Evelyn. She was surprised because she herself was
very different from this central character. Where Evelyn is
cool and controlled, my mother was volatile and hot-
tempered, prone to regular volcanic outbursts. She was also
down-to-earth and hard working. 'In many ways, I'm more
like Lil,' she said in her Lancashire accent, not unlike the
Mancunian one Lil has. She was right. I had to agree. I
thought that perhaps this was another case of exploring in
the fiction something of my own life 'not-experience'. Then,
as I was watching a rehearsal for the 2007 Shared Experience
production, I realised that there were aspects of Evelyn's
highly strung demeanour that reminded me of the occasional
behaviour of my ex-husband, whose parents had, as children,
been refugees with their families from Nazi Germany. Later,
in his teenage years, he had lost his father, elder brother and
mother. I found myself identifying with Faith's position,
trying to appease or alleviate some unexpressed grief or pain,
very possibly troubled with guilt, that I didn't entirely
understand in this person with whom I had been living for
twenty years or more. Perhaps writing the play was a way to

probe, attempt to find some insight into and cope more fully with the psychological dynamics of a husband who had suffered traumatic family loss and still lived with the profound impact of this in ways that he could not express. My creative imagination strove to express these for myself somehow and Evelyn was born from this artistic impulse.

Diana Quick played the role of Evelyn in the 1996 production that transferred from the Palace Theatre, Watford, to the Vaudeville Theatre in London's West End. Diana started acting in the National Youth Theatre, continued through her student days at Oxford, and has acted in productions at the National Theatre, the RSC and the Royal Court, as well as for Red Ladder and Shared Experience. Best known on TV as Julia in *Brideshead Revisited*, she continues to work across film, theatre, radio and TV. When not acting, she directs the Aldeburgh Documentary Festival. She translated and adapted Simone de Beauvoir's *The Woman Destroyed*, contributed to *Fifty Shades of Feminism*, and wrote a family memoir, *A Tug on the Thread*, about the connection between her family's history in India and her choices as an actress.

At the beginning of *A Tug on the Thread*, Diana writes about playing Evelyn:

> We see a woman who, up to now, has seemed very controlled, even dispassionate, crack up to reveal the hurt child inside. Eva has had to grow up far away from her parents, she has made a life for herself and is to all intents a middle-class, middle-aged English woman. The crisis of the play unfolds as we discover that this is far from a successful transformation, for it was made by denying her true identity. She rejects her mother because the cost of reopening those old wounds is too high, but in refusing this opportunity she ruins any chance she has of healing herself.

> As far as I know I am not Jewish, but when I was asked how I went about playing Evelyn it set me thinking. As an actor you fish into any memories, stories, observations you may have collected on your way through life and, if they chime with the situation you are required to act out, you use them. Of course imagination plays a large part, too, but it

always starts with something you feel you know about. For *Kindertransport* I had thought about my own father a great deal. He had been raised in India, and was sent away to a school in the Himalayas aged five. He came to England at seventeen to go to dental school and never went back, barely had any connection with his family again. As I worked on Evelyn I thought about the emotional cost of leaving your family behind; of how my father was very controlled but loving, and yet – like Evelyn – he could also be curiously unapproachable and unknowable.

When Diana and I met again seventeen years after this production, we at once found ourselves discussing the connections that have emerged between the play and her own life story, as well as the actual experiences of members of the audience.

You felt it when you were on stage because of the quality of their listening. But you felt it too afterwards because there were so many people... It was startlingly different to most plays... I mean, there are always a few people who want to say that they had a lovely time or 'Please can I have your autograph?' But the difference was that there were people who really wanted to talk about how it reflected on their own experiences. And so many said that they had never talked about it before – that was very important. Either they were survivors or they were children of survivors, or they were Kinder or children of Kinder, but they'd all had the same thing of not wanting to open up this gigantic can of beans. For the children, like for Faith in the play, it was really, really tough because clearly the parents were very deformed by the experience. Even though Eva/Evelyn has apparently come away and continues to live a productive life, she's terribly damaged and can't ever go back, certainly can't embrace the mother who survives.

It's very difficult to take on a part which is completely unknown to you. Even if the exterior circumstances of the role, like with Evelyn, are very different from one's own experience, the heart of it has to chime with something you recognise. It has to just capture your imagination in some way. I'm a mother and I have a daughter. On top of that, my

family situation was that my father had been sent away from
home as a small child, and I didn't know when I was doing
Kindertransport what that involved exactly. I had a sort of
Lil figure in my life, I had my mother and my grandmother,
who would talk about it a bit, but nobody really wanted to
open up about it. There was a row between my father and
his father when eventually his father came to Britain. His
father had been born and bred in India and didn't come to
Britain until the mid-1950s, and when he came we met him
once – I'd only met him once – and then we didn't see him
any more. The stories that we were told were piecemeal
stories, rather glamorous, about black panthers, grizzly
bears and the jungle. Nothing about heartache and being
estranged from the family or losing his mother. In fact, his
mother died when he was four. I didn't know till I was a
teenager that he'd lost his mother, because there was a
stepmother who we called grandmother even though we
didn't know her. For me, reading your script connected
with things that I already sort of understood about what
sort of complications and silences can exist in families even
when people say they love each other.

We meet little Eva and see her loving relationship with
Helga right at the top of the play, and at the same time we
see the rather painful love between grown-up Evelyn and
her daughter Faith, who's about to leave home, and these
intercut so the one informs the other very clearly. You see
the simple love that Helga has for her child and the simple
love that Eva has for her mother and her confusion at being
sent away. At the same time you see the very complex,
multilayered, inarticulate love between the grown-up
version of the child, Evelyn, and her daughter, Faith, who
wants to love her and also wants to be free. Faith is in a
double-bind because she wants to fly, and at the same time
she can't. And the mother has put her there even though
she's pretending not to, trying so hard not to be needy, but
clearly is. You understand the complexities of it.

I read Primo Levi and I read *Maus* by Art Spiegelman –
graphic novel, fantastic – and David Grossman's *See Under
Love*, and also histories of the Third Reich. It was useful
just to get the historical context because I was so ignorant
about it. I went to a little Christian school and we didn't

study twentieth-century Jewish history. Although I did do the Second World War, but it wasn't focused in on the history of European Jewry in that way. The detail of it was very unfamiliar.

Whatever careful work one does with the script and so on, a lot of one's understanding of a part is intuitive. So I felt that I understood a lot about Evelyn... I assumed that her marriage ended because she was too impenetrable emotionally to sustain it. I imagined that her husband had found someone else who was more responsive. Evelyn was not available, too held in... I understood her love for her adoptive mother. Actually, I think the hardest thing, the really hard thing which took a lot of work, was to play the scene where the adult Evelyn meets Helga.

I can remember the extraordinary attention from the audience every night playing that scene. It's a complete and utter coup. And I don't think it matters whether it's playing in real time or not. It's the emotional truth of it, from both points of view... It couldn't have happened any earlier because I don't think that Evelyn would have been ready to articulate what she actually says. It's the hardest scene to understand, and that's because it's so shocking to have a child say, 'I would rather have taken my chances... I would rather have died with you... rather than being sent away.' That's where I really had to use what I knew already of the character from working on the earlier part of the play, and then use my imagination because I grew up in the bosom of a very warm and loving family. And also not having that Jewish heritage, that collective guilt, which I now understand much better, of being a survivor and thinking, 'Why me? Why have I survived when everybody else is gone?' All that was very difficult to comprehend at the time because I hadn't really come across it before... I understand why one might feel that it would have been better to have stayed with your family and received whatever fate had in store for you. I think one can understand it intellectually, yes of course you want to be with your blood family, but then that deeper level of feeling that if you had been with them and survived then you wouldn't need to feel guilty about surviving... Of course, if she had, knowing what I know now in so much more detail about what happened in the camps, the chances are that Eva wouldn't have survived because she was a child – she would have just gone into the queue that went straight into the ovens.

Evelyn truly loves Lil. At some cost to herself and by an effort of will, she has replaced Helga with Lil. That's part of why, finally, in confrontation with Helga as an adult, she says, 'You're not my mother. You gave me away.' Love is an action. In the end, however much in one's gut you want to be with your blood parent, and however good the reasoning is from that person that you're safer by being sent away, the experience of the child is that you're abandoned, you're sent to the unknown, and the abyss is all around you and you might fall in. Then somebody arrives who loves you in an uncomplicated way and sticks with you and raises you and shows you a way to live your life – that's the action, that's the loving action for the child.

I can understand the Ratcatcher intellectually because the story of the Pied Piper of Hamelin is something that Eva has brought with her from Germany, and is connected to her mother and storytelling. And the idea of something you might fall into and never be able to climb out of. But the Ratcatcher is very ambiguous. He's as scary as he is reassuring. Is she a rat? Is Eva the rat who's going to be caught? I think that the play is informed by the idea of what must have happened to everybody who was Jewish in Europe living through the Third Reich, which is that you are prey and you are going to be got… So, the Ratcatcher can be hostile, but also he might be catching the other rats. I never really understood that, to tell you the truth: whether he is friend or foe, because he comes as this night terror into her life.

Evelyn says to her daughter, 'I'd rather die than go back.' And I felt that, I understood that so much better in the course of the run from what people were saying at the stage door, about being survivors. I had many very powerful conversations, but there was one woman who made a huge impression and who, by the time she came to the play, was now able to talk about her experiences. She and her brother had both survived the death camps and had come to England after the war. Brother and sister had never discussed what had happened to them, either with each other or with their children. This woman's daughter, who came to the play with her, was now a pychotherapist. Through her training, the daughter had acquired a vocabulary that enabled her to discuss her mother's issues, and she had said, 'Mum, you really have got to talk about what happened to you, because otherwise the time will pass and we will never know what you have been through.' The mother said, 'I can't talk about it because if I talk about it, or even if I let myself think about it, I get ill.' And the daughter said, 'Well, what happens to you if you don't talk about it?' She said, 'I just feel guilty. I feel guilty as hell.' And the daughter said to her, 'Well, Mum, if you're ill, you can be treated, but if you keep all that wretched guilt bottled up inside you, no one can help you.' She had eventually persuaded her mother to start to speak about what her experiences had been. And indeed she had a series of illnesses and had to be treated medically for quite a long time. But eventually she went through all of that and it was cathartic for her, and then she was able to bear witness to what her life had actually been, to the point where by the time I met her she was now going into schools and teaching about what had happened. This was a huge shift, helped by her daughter, by her daughter's love and also by her daughter's professional expertise. Evelyn doesn't have that. She's just got Lil, and she's got the slightly inarticulate love of Faith.

As an actor, the task is to understand the development of the character. It's not just to follow the narrative. It's what happens to your character, so that you come on, stuff happens and then you're different by the end. You do that within a scene, within an act and you do it through the whole play. You take the audience through that story with you as you experience the character's change before their eyes.

And presumably Faith is going away now. And that's the growth, the maturity. Evelyn allows her to go, even though she's going to be abandoned again. However much she feels that it's necessary, it's going to be at great cost to her… I don't think she feels desperate. She feels determined. She's a strong woman, isn't she? What I worry about for her is that so much of what she does is through will… She knows what must happen, but the child in Evelyn is never healed. You know, even in that scene with Helga, I don't think it's really a resolution. It moves her forward because she's able to articulate finally what she really felt about it. But she can't go back and be with her mother and experience family life. She was sent away as a nine-year old–into a strange land where she didn't know the language or anybody. I'm not sure at the end whether Evelyn has really moved on from that and decided to let that be, which is what one has to do with so much of the stuff that happens in life.

I've found that as human beings we can hold a lot of different relationships, and they don't cancel each other out. That's what you've got in the play. She loves the mother that she can't be with. She loves Lil. She loves Faith, but she has to let her go. I think what has changed as well at the end for Evelyn is that she forgives Helga. I think that at the beginning of the play when they're in the attic there's an air of martyrdom about Evelyn. She doesn't actually express it, but Faith picks up on it, which is why she can't go: 'I'm not going to go.' By the end, I think that's gone. I think it's more full-hearted, her being able to let Faith move on. And it's because she's articulated something about herself. She's brought into consciousness… even if she hadn't known it… but she's articulated what she felt towards Helga. She knows more than intellectually that children must set forth and find their own way.

So, in the final moment, it still hurts, but it's a hurt which is supportable… We did have a huge shadow of the Ratcatcher coming over the back of the cyclorama [a large curtain or wall, often concave, at the back of a stage]. She has to be the grown-up in that situation. It's a true thing, you know, she can do it. But I don't know what happens when Faith goes away, and Lil goes away, and she's all alone. She probably doesn't cry. But there's a bleakness inside, a bleakness in her soul. Because she is essentially alone. But it is not hopeless.

Eva and Evelyn

'I find the script really intriguing, especially with two
Eva/Evelyns.' *Rebecca Waas, theatre director*

'At the innermost core of loneliness is a deep and powerful
yearning for union with one's lost self.' *Brendan Francis*

'Every year, when you're a child, you become a
different person.' *Alice Munro*

Whilst researching for *Kindertransport* I was working as an
Education Officer at the Unicorn Theatre, whose remit was
to mount productions for five- to twelve-year-olds. The work
ranged from serious drama to light-hearted musical enter-
tainment, wildly imaginative and inventive sometimes, more
everyday at others. The validity of 'theatre for children' as a
distinct form is sometimes questioned within professional
theatre circles, especially when it is invariably written and
produced by adults, but one thing that did distinguish each
and every one of these plays from most other drama was that
the central character was always a child.

At the same time I was regularly attending art-therapy sessions, in which I would paint, as I felt it, 'like a child'. I had
no training as an artist and had given up the subject early in
secondary school. So I played freely, not minding whether it
was 'any good', simply messing around with watercolours or
poster paints, crayons and chalks, on different kinds of paper.
What I accessed by being around lots of children and engag-
ing regularly with my own play was a sense of open curiosity
and enthusiasm alongside a certain vulnerability, a sense of
living each moment in the present and feeling everything
keenly; also of learning how things work by watching and
doing. So when I started to write *Kindertransport*, I couldn't

help but be drawn to the child Eva's perspective as much as to the adult Evelyn's. What hit me almost at once was how distant the two were from one another. I wanted to evoke the viewpoint of each one separately from their decades apart in the timeless place that connected them as one person. So telling their stories independently, in parallel, and exploring how they invisibly intersect, became the natural framework for the play.

The laws that govern the employment of children in live theatre are strict, limiting their hours and requiring extra provision, including chaperones. So, casting a child is more costly than employing an adult. Also, if the role is a demanding one, then it's useful to draw on the level of expertise and skill that a trained adult professional is likely to have. In the first productions, the director Abigail Morris chose to cast an actor as close in age as was feasible, given the various professional constraints, because she wanted to tap into the authentic energy of a child on stage in the role. In most other professional productions, adult actors, typically in their late teens or early twenties, are usually cast to play Eva.

In the Shared Experience production that toured Britain in 2007, the role of Eva was played by Matti Houghton, alongside Marion Bailey as Evelyn. Polly Teale directed them in the physically expressive, stylised signature mode of the company.

Marion Bailey was born in Harrow, Middlesex, and has always lived in London. She has worked since 1974 in theatre, film, TV and radio. She was a member of the National Youth Theatre and trained at the Guildhall School of Music & Drama. She has worked extensively in theatres across the UK, including the National Theatre, the Royal Court, the Old Vic, Hampstead, the Tricycle, the Bush, Chichester, Bristol Old Vic, Edinburgh's Royal Lyceum, the West Yorkshire Playhouse and in London's West End. Her first job was as an Acting/ASM at Oldham Rep. She is possibly best known for her work with the writer/director Mike Leigh, both on film and in the theatre. She was nominated for a Best Supporting Actress by the TMA Theatre Awards for her role as Evelyn in *Kindertransport*. She has one daughter, the actress Alice Bailey Johnson.

Matti Houghton trained at the Guildhall School of Music & Drama. She has had regular work in both theatre and TV. She has worked at many theatres, including the HighTide Festival, Royal & Derngate, the Arcola, the Royal Shakespeare Company, Liverpool Everyman, the Old Vic Tunnels, the Royal Exchange Manchester, the Royal Court and the National Theatre.

Six years after working together in *Kindertransport*, both actors immediately recalled the intensity of the piece. Here are extracts from their conversation about playing two aspects of the same character.

Approaching the Roles

MATTI. For me it was an emotional job.

MARION. Yes, the depth of the emotion was huge because we were going into very dark territory and, of course, it was curious to be on stage with someone else playing the same character. I have done it once before in a play, with someone playing the inner life of the character; but we weren't really doing that, we were playing the same character at different stages of their life…

MATTI.…and completely separate in a way. There's never ever a scene where they meet. We were in the rehearsal room all the time together because that was the Shared Experience process, but the change that happens between what I (as Eva) was doing to what you (as Evelyn) were doing is massive. For you there was a level of emotional repression and for me there were outbursts.

MARION. I suppose that I do think about it as being on stage with that character's inner life. There was that raging child before me. She was always there. My character was quite an uptight, respectable English woman who didn't fling her emotions around readily.

Uptight is too strong, I think, but if you met her you would meet someone very restrained and careful with her words. And out of the corner of my eye, as her inner life, was this raging child full of terrible emotions that hadn't been integrated. And, of course, the territory itself is very, very dark. I was born in the 1950s and the older I've got the more aware I've become that just before my birth had been this terrible trauma in Europe that my parents had been through. As a kid I used to play on bomb sites on the way home from school. The Kodak factory nearby used to test their air-raid siren every so often and I can remember this mournful wailing. I can remember Mrs Marchant, our neighbour, who was a middle-aged Jewish lady with two sons... It's only now that I look back and think, 'My God, what had they been through?' All that darkness that still hangs over Europe. My generation went out and partied hard to try and compensate for that awful darkness. All of that is involved with this play.

MATTI. I was twenty-two when I played Eva and it was maybe my third job out of drama school. I found out that I was playing Eva the day before we started rehearsals and I remember having to do a readthrough, and being young I jumped in and did all the changes of accent and all that kind of thing in front of the entire room, and I remember that being a real thing. I remember just having complete terror, speaking German. You just dive in. With Shared Experience the whole thing with the process is that from the very first day you either go for it or you don't, and if you don't then you're going to have a lot of trouble working with them. We as a company just completely did it. For me, in terms of process and courage it was a really great job. I learned a lot from everyone, just diving in head first, all-embracing.

Accents

MATTI. Eva has quite a lot of scenes in German at first and then they get fewer and fewer and then her German accent fades. Then she reaches the age of seventeen and then you have that brilliant thing of her being too English.

MARION. There's something about the German language that lends itself to very precise English. What I was aiming for was to find something that was just a little bit too precise, a little bit formal. She has an uprightness, and a carefulness, and I suppose that comes out of having to be something you're not.

MATTI. We met a woman who had come from Germany as a child and she had a really precise English accent. I felt, because there's so much accent change, that if I'd added in a bit of Manchester it would have muddied the whole thing to get from that to what Marion was doing. Everything is choice for Evelyn – how she walks, how she talks. It's not real. It's slightly manufactured because she's denying something very deep within.

MARION. I made a decision that, because as a child she would still have her German accent, perhaps she'd had elocution lessons or something in order to completely stop anybody ever asking where she came from. This is a woman who decides to make herself accentless and no one is going to ask the question. I don't think that she would have acquired a Manchester accent.

MATTI. Yeah. It's not natural. Whereas if she had just grown up in Manchester then of course she'd fit in by doing that.

MARION. It's never quite fluid. You wouldn't spot that if you met Evelyn. It would just be something about the way she spoke, so she might seem slightly overly formal.

Being a Swan

MARION. We worked on finding the animal that best represented our character and I blindly picked a swan.

MATTI. A swan, yeah.

MARION. We both did it independently. Swans are incredibly powerful and strong. They kill to protect their young. You wouldn't pick a fight with a swan. There's also a regal, upright, again rather careful elegance which I wanted.

MATTI. And underneath a swan, the legs are working and working…

MARION. ...to keep yourself going. So on the surface is this serenity and in the lower depths you're absolutely going berserk. The fear and terror...

MATTI. That was kind of the division of the part...

MARION. I found it useful anyway thinking of a swan. I don't always think of an animal when I'm working on a character, but Shared Experience has a very physical rehearsal process and so it did help. I don't think I could remember any other animal when anyone has asked me to do this before, but this has stayed with me as an image.

MATTI. I think it was the underneath, what she's struggling to be and achieve, and there are not many animals where...

MARION. She's a fighter as well.

MATTI. I guess when you're looking at animals you take one particular thing that might key you into that character, and the fight underneath, the struggle of working out who you are, who you want to be. Also, the big thing with her is the fight not to let go, and then suddenly she does let go. Then once she's let go, she can't go back.

Younger and Older

MATTI. Everything that she knows or knew, her parents, culture, and love, and connection to her past, she has to let go. That moment at the train station when she realises that they're not coming and she goes to the train guard and she has that conversation, 'They're not on the train, they're not on the train.' That breakdown. In our production that was quite a moment, like a real tantrum, a big meltdown. It was like everything that had been happening suddenly came out. Then in the following scene, the transition, I took off all the jewellery and put it all away, which is the last thing that she has connecting her to her mother, and from then on it's about how you rebuild. Then that scene where she meets her mother and she can't accept her back into her life. So, that really interesting thing of those moments when you cut something off and then once you've made that decision you can't go back.

MARION. Evelyn says to Faith, 'I can't go back.'

MATTI. That was always so helpful, because you normally think, 'I wonder what this character would be like in twenty or thirty years time.' And of course you have access to what your character turns in to, which is an amazing tool.

MARION. And the same for me in thinking, 'What was her childhood like?'

MATTI. Feels very helpful in terms of discovery.

MARION. I can remember watching you play Eva, so that we could both depict the same person albeit at different times of their life. We didn't try to do it literally. It was just to indicate it in a way. It was more important for us to find vocal, physical, facial mannerisms. And actually that happens symbiotically somehow, just by being on the stage at the same time, knowing you're being the same person. It's not necessarily a conscious thing, but as long as you're aware and work together with someone, you can find yourself physically working with someone in the same rhythm and movement.

MATTI. And you're also in the room. In a different rehearsal process we might have rehearsed our scenes separately, but we were all in, all the time for six weeks. It really helped in terms of language. We were all speaking the same language physically, on the same page.

MARION. We had your young self, your older self, your inner self all on the stage at the same time, which was extraordinary, because normally as an actor you are depicting a character and trying to show the audience, trying to indicate the inner life. With this, we almost didn't have to, because the inner life is actually on stage with you. All you have to do, as I was playing Evelyn, is simply depict her external condition until the very end, because the audience can actually see what is going on inside her and what was going on from her youth. So you couldn't muddy the waters as an actor by trying to give too much. You had to stay with whatever it was that Evelyn was on the surface, what she was trying to present to the world.

Rejecting Helga

MARION. You can't make moral judgements. You have to understand Evelyn's character. This is a woman who is what she is because of the guilt and what she can't acknowledge. It's only the next worse thing... yes, the next worse thing to denying your own child is to deny your mother, I guess. She can't forgive herself. Whether she ever does is another question. Certainly, in my depiction of her the breakdown at the end is the beginning of a process where she can start to forgive herself on some level. The whole reason that she cannot acknowledge her past is because of that one thing, that one terrible, terrible thing. I can understand it absolutely.

MATTI. It was about survival.

MARION. Yes, she had to survive and that's how she did it. Bless her heart, she was a little child. Children in war go through the most terrible things, and she was a victim as much as anyone else. If she was a real person, then I'd hope that one day she'd learn to love herself and forgive herself for that action because what else could she have done to survive it? It's too big a thing.

MATTI. And also, Helga won't come to England, so she also denies her daughter. I think that that's slightly overlooked by the audience, because you've followed Eva so you're with her story and you see it as her decision not to go with Helga. But Helga doesn't choose to stay where Eva is. So the decision is a joint one.

MARION. It's too much to ask of a child. It's a common thing in adoption, I suppose. The thing of tracing the birth parent and then feeling guilt because you choose your adoptive parents, because they're the ones who brought you up, loved you and you love them. And then there's this other being suddenly and you're helpless if you just don't feel it by then.

MATTI. There's been so much removal. It's so hard, because she thought her parents were dead and you work so hard to remove that in order to move on, because otherwise you can't move on. Then for someone to come back into your life and expect something of you, it's just unthinkable. A very, very difficult scene to play, because…

MARION.…because of what you know the mother has survived. That's what makes it so awful.

MATTI. Yes.

MARION. That's life. It's not that anybody is a monster or a demon. It's just the way it's happened.

MATTI. You think about what you do when you're seventeen, the decisions you make, all those things… and… you're just trying to live.

MARION. You're looking for a mother and you find a mother, then another mother comes and you're pushed back. What do you do? You get on with your life.

MATTI. Pandora [Pandora Colin, who portrayed Helga in the 2007 tour] and I played that whole scene just looking out at the port, and we had very, very little eye contact for the entire scene. It was great to have those passages where you just couldn't engage with each other, because if you could engage then maybe your decisions about what to do would be different. We couldn't bear to look at each other, actually, which is what happens.

MARION. But also that scene was played out when I was on stage, which meant that I actually had that memory in my mind's eye, literally in front of me. Normally, I'd be standing in the wings trying to create that memory in my head in order to go on and play the next bit. I didn't have to in this production because there it was being played out on stage in front of me. It made it much easier.

The Ending

MARION. At the very end of Act Two, when the breakdown happens for Evelyn, then we connected. It was a huge relief. I can remember feeling this, not just because we'd come to the end of this journey, which was quite a tough one to take, but I remember it was wonderful just to finally look Eva in the eye.

MATTI. There's a bit earlier, right at the end of Act One, when Evelyn says, 'Don't worry, I'll protect you. I won't let him get you. You're safe with me.' Something like that, but we didn't connect then, because the moment at the end of Act Two was so big.

MARION. Actually she can't protect her. It's a lie when she says that she can protect her at the end of Act One. It's really a moment of denial when she says, 'Don't worry don't worry don't worry, everything's fine! Don't panic!' It's only when she's gone through everything in Act Two that she can finally acknowledge this child and the experience she's had. That child is going to suffer torment in eternity until the adult can turn round and acknowledge the child's pain. That's when you begin your journey to sanity and health, if you're lucky. That doesn't happen till the end of the play. My memory of the end of the play is just us together. That's the heightened point of the play. The whole play has been leading up to this moment.

MATTI. I was definitely on stage.

MARION. Together in the same room, and that's the end of the journey. (*To Matti.*) You used to look at me, I used to look at you, and that was the moment of acknowledgement.

MATTI. It's the previous scene with Helga, that's the big transition moment for Eva into Evelyn...

MARION. Into adulthood.

MATTI. Yeah, into adulthood, and that concludes with the connection that we made on stage. Before that, when Evelyn confronts Helga and says that she really wanted to die with her, I think that she's saying it for Eva as well because that last scene with Helga is so cold, in a brilliant way, and I remember just loving that scene because it felt so stark. Then going into the emotional breakdown of that character you get an extra release from that scene which is so cold. She's turned into Evelyn.

MARION. Eva is very much there during the Evelyn/Helga scene. The thing that's happening between Evelyn and her birth mother is absolutely about her childhood, her inner child. So she had to be there in our style of production.

MATTI. I don't think I left the stage once. During one performance, I came on stage after the interval and I was meant to have all the jewellery, and I remember realising that I hadn't got it. I had to go offstage, right upstairs to the dressing room, get the jewellery and come back on stage.

MARION. My heart was beating, 'Where's she gone where's she gone, where's she gone?'

MATTI. Because I had to be there all the time, and so did you. To go from being nine years old to fifteen and seventeen, I just changed my shoes on stage, took the jewellery off, and I remember having a really hard time getting that transition.

MARION. I remember that your physicality changed. It was brilliant in terms of acting a slightly older person. It didn't really need a costume change.

MATTI. The whole production was very simple in terms of costume. That was great because it's enabling for an actor and you know that the director trusts that you'll be able to make it all work rather than needing a wig or whatever.

MARION. You could see this child.

MATTI. It was one of those moments for me. You have them once in every production if you're lucky, those moments where you're working and working and working and you can't get to it, you can't get something, and then I remember I was going over and over the scene and I don't know what happened, something just clicked and that was it. I can't even say what the thought was, what changed, but something just clicked and I knew that was the right choice about how to make that age thing work.

MARION. I remember when the lights went off and the blackout at the end of the play, we were both on stage and having to find our position for the curtain call.

MATTI. We were both there together at the end.

Marion Bailey as Evelyn and Pandora Colin as Helga in the 2007 Shared Experience
production © Donald Cooper/Photostage

Helga

'Children are the anchors that hold a mother to life.'
Sophocles

'I need my mother to set a good example and be a person I can respect, but in most matters she's an example of what *not* to do.'
Anne Frank

The mother-in-law that I never met was called Hella. In adulthood, she was a close friend of Rena who talked to me so generously about coming to London as a child refugee. Hella also originally hailed from Hamburg and had been the sister of Eva, whom I met in later life in Israel and whose childhood school photo had inspired me to name my central character after her. Eva and Hella had grown up together with their parents in Jerusalem. Hella moved to Britain as a young woman, where she became the mother of the man to whom I was married for twenty years. Hella had died when he, her only remaining son, was nineteen years old. Her husband had died a few years earlier, leaving her a widow and single parent. Her eldest son had died suddenly in his early twenties, almost exactly a year before her own death. The loss experienced by this one surviving son to whom I was married was a hidden yet powerful presence in his life, a haunting echo of the German Jewish heritage he embodied, and so, in naming the character in the play who is the German mother who loses so much and somehow survives the war in Europe, I paid homage to Hella. Acknowledging that this character was my own creation, different in age, experience and personal qualities from the real woman I had never known personally, I adjusted her name to Helga.

In the second draft of *Kindertransport*, Helga delivered a monologue at the beginning of the play that preceded the 'sewing on the button' scene with Eva. In early drafts, it is important for a writer to write whatever pours onto the page, not censoring a word. In these initial sketches, overstatement is common as the writer works out the shape, motives, qualities, etc., of a character. The craft of redrafting requires selecting the significant elements from this material and then embedding the feelings, attitudes and fears implicitly into the dramatic action, or the 'subtext', of the dialogue. What goes unsaid is often far more powerful than what is explicitly revealed, and as the rewrites are themselves rewritten and rewritten, the text is honed, layers added and interwoven to create a textured character that is operating on many levels, inner and outer. This monologue was cut and does not appear in the third draft of the play. The sense of what Helga expresses here is ingrained as subtext in the current version in the dialogue between her and Eva about sewing on the button, during the packing of the case and the telling of the Ratcatcher story.

KINDERTRANSPORT —
SECOND DRAFT, CIRCA 1992

Act One, Scene One

HELGA *stands alone. She is elegant and well turned-out. She contains her emotions with well-formed phrases and good elocution. She is tightly lit. The rest of the stage is hidden in the dark.*

As HELGA *speaks, a haunting pipe tune fills the air.*

HELGA. Tomorrow I will put my daughter onto a train. Then I will leave her there. On her own. In twenty-four hours I will still be here and she will be speeding away from me. I can sense the emptiness of her absence already.

Pause.

I do not want to do it.

Pause.

I do not want to lose her. Yet I do it for precisely that reason – not to lose her. Short-term sentiment is not appropriate any more. The long term looms over us all and hers must be secured. My grandfather wore a black coat and hat and talked in sayings. 'You are my children. You are my jewels.' Well, my jewels must be banked abroad, safe in some other person's treasury.

Pause.

What would you do if you were in prison? What would you do if you saw an open window high up? Climb through? But the window's too small for you. Only your child will fit through. Make her climb! Go on, make her! Hear her scream or silently sob when you're not looking or, worst of all, put on a brave face to save your feelings. Don't cling to your child. Don't be possessive. There's life in losing her. Are you a bad parent or a good one?

Pause.

What is happening to us all? Parents protecting their children by sending them into the hands of people who might despise and misunderstand them. Are we not failures, we mothers and fathers? Our children are safer with strangers than they are with us. I am so impotent that I will deport my only daughter with gratitude in my heart. 'You are my children. You are my immortality. You are my hope.' Let the children lead us all out of the abyss.

EVA*'s voice comes out of the darkness.*

EVA. What's an abyss, Mutti?

*

Over the years I have seen a number of actresses play Helga with tremendous skill and understatement, bringing their own distinctive quality to the role, highlighting her self-possession whilst evoking different levels of warmth and coolness. In each case, the transformation from the mannered, elegant woman speaking immaculately at the beginning of the play (when Helga and Evelyn speak together in their native German, the most effective convention is to use an English 'received pronunciation' accent), to the depleted, harrowed, ghost-like figure with her thick German accent at the end of the play, has been shocking.

Three actresses here reflect on their experiences of playing the role.

Ruth Mitchell

Ruth has played Helga three times, in the Soho Theatre productions in 1993 and 1996, and for a BBC Radio 4 version. As a classical actor, Ruth toured the world with the Royal Shakespeare Company and for three years was part of Katie Mitchell's ensemble at The Other Place. She also played roles as diverse as the title role in *Hamlet* and Virginia Woolf in Robin Brooks' adaptation of *Orlando*. She has also created her own show, which investigates identity and ancestry, inspired by the Plymouth Synagogue, the oldest Ashkenazi synagogue in continuous use in the English-speaking world.

> It was a fantastically raw emotional show that had amazing parts for women. Helga was this beautiful middle-class German woman who at the beginning had everything and ended up with nothing. We do not know what she had to do in order to survive, but it certainly changed her and she becomes quite single-minded. This was a marvellous story arc for me to undergo. I loved the emotional pull that Helga's reveal had on the audience, loved being so chic at the beginning. I was also aware that I was playing a German and felt a need to be as authentic as I could be. When I was given a second chance to play Helga, I was able to investigate this harsher aspect of her story. I think my interpretation may have been stronger the second time, although overall I preferred the first performances, because it was so new and we didn't know the impact it was going to have.
>
> I certainly tried to develop a story for her survival. I read Primo Levi. It was hard research but gave me a huge insight into what people had to do in order to survive, and that many then couldn't live with the guilt afterwards.

I went through storylines such as – she had sex with a guard in order to survive; she had a talent that kept her alive, maybe typing letters or another administrative skill; she stole from other inmates.

I loved my costume in the first production, a fitted two-piece suit and a beautiful wig, which made me feel very feminine. I never really came to terms with the fact that Helga arrives in England to meet Eva again and looks like a refugee. I remember thinking that logistically her hair would be longer in the time frame we were dealing with, and that as a proud woman who was once a happy middle-class wife and mother she would have made more of an effort when meeting her child again. But I realised that, for emotional effect, the refugee look worked and she had to now resemble the Ratcatcher figure and look totally different from the first time we saw her.

I had to keep very focused, especially in Helga's latter scenes, because they had such an emotional effect on the audience. Being in a small, intimate space like the Cockpit Theatre in London meant we could hear all the weeping that happened, and sometimes the sound coming from the audience was a collective wail, as if people had been trying to hold back their cries inside but could not physically restrain them.

This was upsetting to hear, especially because I felt I had to be truthful and not allow the 'actor' in me to wallow in the emotion. Those scenes were very upsetting to play, but one can easily understand why Eva rejects her mother as she feels she was rejected herself. And when Helga comes back, she's so brittle and damaged, it's probably impossible for Eva to grasp that her mother did what she did out of love.

Working on Helga's final scenes was both liberating and difficult in equal measure. The emotional outpouring was a gift for an actor but the angst behind the words was difficult. The first time I played her, I very much played the pity card, but the second time I tried to go for a harder approach – what had she gone through? What had she done to survive and how had that changed her? There is a big question underlying the scene: Helga says, 'We have all done bad things', and Eva asks, 'What did you do?', but

Helga changes the subject. This unanswered question is a
real hook for me in this scene, and even though the
sympathy seems to be with Helga, there are flashes of anger
or impatience that she can show that are also personality
changes. This is the underlying tragedy that what these
people have gone through has changed them for ever and
there seems to be no going back. She always promised she
would come back and she is so thrown by the fact that Eva
didn't believe that.

One of the hardest things to hear is that Eva has changed
her name to an English one – that is somehow a real kick in
the teeth. The parent gives the child a name, in this case,
from her grandmother, so there is a family continuation and
that gets changed. This is interesting in the light of what I
am currently working on, a project about identity and
heritage. When names get changed, history gets papered
over and sent down other pathways, and is therefore harder
to trace. I found it hard as I thought Eva could have gone
along with her mother to spare her feelings, maybe allowed
her mother to call her by her German name; but she
reminds Helga of her new name a second time in the scene,
as if Eva is now changing the subject when she can't answer
the question asked of her.

I remember thinking at the time: how could Evelyn have
kept it all from her daughter? But having gone through my
own family tree with my father, it's amazing what people
keep to themselves, and I'm not even talking about events
as traumatic as those that Evelyn went through.

The scene with Evelyn was different to all the other scenes,
an un-naturalistic scene, a cathartic opening-up for Evelyn,
hearing her side after years of holding it in. When she
proclaims, 'Didn't it ever occur to you that I might have
wanted to die with you?' I think that's something people
aren't prepared for and yet is the most unselfish question to
hear – it hits really hard, that question, and you find
yourself saying, 'Yes, of course, these children have lived
with the guilt of surviving too.' Helga has a guilt but it is a
guilt that came out of something proactive, whereas these
children had no say in their guilt. That is such a hard thing
to hear and Eva/Evelyn becomes so human and childlike at
that point. I have to say this scene was almost a child's game

of one-upmanship – 'my suffering was greater', etc. But easy to do after the overwhelming hurt of the previous scene, as if years of grief can be wiped clean by getting one better. I don't know, that makes it sound trivial but there was a great sense of, 'You don't know what I went through.' This really hit a nerve with audience members, the words of a grown woman to her mother spoken with childish inflection was very truthful and hard to hear.

I feel very honoured to have been part of the first production, it felt special at the time to tell a story that gives a different take on the war, through the eyes of a child, and through the eyes of women and mothers. It makes you think about your own family and possible secrets. It makes you question what you would do to save your children. The Jewish audience really took it to their hearts, but the themes of mother/daughter relationships are universal. Even now, twenty years later, if people find out I was in the first production, they are always interested to know that, especially teachers who are using the text. Reliving the emotion does not diminish it, in fact, the older one gets, the more emotional it feels.

Pandora Colin

Pandora played Helga in the 2007 Shared Experience national tour of *Kindertransport*. She has a young son and her work as an actor spans theatre, TV, radio and film. Theatre work includes *The Dark Earth and the Light Sky* and *The House of Bernada Alba* at the Almeida Theatre, and plays at the National Theatre, Trafalgar Studios, Theatre503, King's Head, Edinburgh Festival, Salisbury Playhouse, Bath Theatre Royal, Sheffield Crucible and the Arcola. Her work for TV includes *Mr Selfridge*, *Titanic* and *Hotel Babylon*.

My first impression of *Kindertransport* was that it spoke honestly about what families do to and for each other, and that it had so many fantastic, complex parts for women. It explores the lengths people will go to in order to protect their loved ones; the emotional/psychological legacy of war on families and society; the innate kindness and capacity of love that many humans have; and how traumatic experience can prevent people from having the ability to emotionally communicate in a healthy way in further relationships.

Helga seems tough, and even heartless, but she's doing what she thinks is best to save her daughter, and then to survive her decisions and their fallout. Also, having lived through the camps, there is a strength of will that we glimpse in her sacrificing her happiness to save her daughter at the beginning, that she now possesses in order to survive herself.

Playing someone who makes strong, bold, sometimes brutal decisions is a fascinating challenge, and also playing someone who does things that some might find make her unsympathetic, but helping an audience to understand that she does it all as a result of fear and love.

She has to make decisions that one can only imagine having to make, so it's a challenge finding the truth of that. We all did lengthy and detailed improvisations about her family life before the play starts, and also of any incidents that are referred to in the play that have happened offstage so that we had a physical memory of them.

Those final scenes were very upsetting to play, but one can easily understand why Eva rejects her mother as she feels she was rejected herself, and when Helga comes back, she's so brittle and damaged, it's probably impossible for Eva to grasp that her mother did what she did out of love.

We all got letters from and spoke to people who had been in the Kindertransport, and their responses were very touching. Audience reactions were on the whole very positive. We did question-and-answer sessions throughout the tour and they were very moving, because so many people had themselves come over in the Kindertransport and felt that the play was very accurate. Some people who had not been in the Kindertransport couldn't accept that the mother and daughter didn't stay together once they found each other, and even though we told them there were cases of this happening, they found that difficult to accept.

Jane Kaczmarek

A graduate of the Yale School of Drama and an accomplished theatre actress, Jane has also received a number of Golden Globe and Emmy nominations for her role as Lois in the TV comedy series *Malcolm in the Middle*. Jane played Helga in the US premiere of *Kindertransport* at the Manhattan Theatre Club, Off-Broadway, New York, in 1994. She then went on to reprise the role in Los Angeles at the Tiffany Theater in 1996. She returned to play Helga for a third time for L.A. Theatre Works' 2013 audio production, recorded in front of a live audience.

> It was a very different experience acting [in *Kindertransport*] for radio as the actors were unable to look at each other due to the demands of recording into the microphones. In some ways it was very freeing. Staring into the blackness of the theatre unfettered my imagination and I was able to conjure like crazy. On the other hand, an actor gets her energy from the other actor in the scene, and listening became more difficult and thus more important than ever.

> Playing Helga three times, through three very different times in my life, is a gift that no other role has afforded me. Age and experience and loss filled me with more emotion than any research could. My daughters – at the time fifteen and ten years old – came to see the play and, driving home, they resoundingly agreed they'd rather die with me than be sent away as Eva was.

> I am a great fan of classical music and know what a huge part of life it was in many Jewish families, especially for the generations before the war. When playing Helga in New York in 1994, I listened to (and I know this is not classical, in fact is from a contemporary mass) 'Pie Jesu' from Andrew Lloyd Webber's *Requiem*. There is a simplicity, a prayer-like quality of a child that I found very moving. Keep in mind this was twenty years ago and the piece was new and not as familiar as it is now. Although, listening to Anna Netrebko sing, it is still divine. By the time we moved on to LA in 1996, I had moved on to Mahler, the third movement of the *Fourth Symphony*. Only the first

minutes, while it is sombre and still, then rising to a heartbreaking crescendo. This piece took me on Helga's train/memory ride through the devastation of Europe and the stillness… on her way to Eva, certain that, 'Home is inside you, inside you and me, it is not a place.' I would listen on a Walkman (remember this was the 1990s!) when Evelyn started her 'I remember books, rows and rows…' and had a backstage person tap me when it was time for my entrance. This was very helpful to achieve a state of fogginess, of being disorientated and fearful when entering the final scene with Eva.

When I did the play this year for L.A. Theatre Works, we collected images of the Kinder and projected them on a screen above and behind the actors. They played on a slideshow as Schumann's *Songs from Childhood: Foreign Lands and Far Away Places* accompanied them. This was the opening of the play, with Helga and Eva beginning their scene as the photos and the music subsided. This piece possesses a feeling of nostalgia and hope, and I think it was very effective in lulling the audience into believing everything is going to be all right with Eva and her family. Raising the stakes on the side of hope gave us (and the audience) so much farther to plunge as the story is told. No one can believe it is going to get this bad, not even when it actually happens. We used Schubert's *Serenade* at the end of Act One and into the intermission and again as the play ended. It was very effective.

Also, I had a nightly ritual before going on stage. I took a moment to be still and ask that the spirit of a woman, a mother, who perished in the camps be with me as I became Helga. I asked only that she give me permission that I honour her loss and be truthful on stage. Maybe because I am not Jewish and that my family is Polish Catholic, it was very important to me to be respectful to those real people who inspired Helga and to all the millions who weren't as fortunate as she.

This character has played a seminal role in my career as an actress.

*

The way in which Eva/Evelyn rejects Helga is often met with disquiet or disbelief. Readers and audiences question the validity of this choice. Yet, in cases where parents did somehow survive, especially when the children sent away were younger, it was more common than not that the relationship between parent and child was irreparably damaged. As one of the Kinder, Ruth Barnett, recalls, reunions were not easy. She had settled into her third foster family at the farm and was in her teens when she experienced an unexpected arrival.

> Then suddenly in 1949 my mother appeared out of nowhere.
>
> Grown-ups did all the arranging and they told you. I was simply told, 'This is your mother.' I didn't recognise her after ten years. She didn't speak a word of English. I didn't speak a word of German. I was actually frightened because I wasn't sure whether she was a real person or a ghost. I remember touching her to see if she was solid. I mean, I was a very... I don't know... naive, little fourteen-year-old compared to fourteen-year-olds today.
>
> We had had occasional letters through the Red Cross from our dad but we didn't hear a single squeak from our mother for ten years. I thought she must be dead. That's what a small child does. It's unbearable that Mummy chooses to be somewhere else, and if she's dead she can't be 'here' and she can't be with anybody else either.
>
> She came over to England and I experienced it as her coming suddenly out of the blue, but I'm sure it was arranged. I just wasn't told until I met her. 'This is your mother and she's going to take you back with her to Germany.' I just couldn't cope with this because for ten years I'd been thoroughly brainwashed with British propaganda, all of which I swallowed. Every day on the news, in the newspaper, in the comics I read, everything was about nasty Nazis and what a terrible place Germany was. So no way was I going to go to Germany.
>
> My brother was seventeen. They didn't intend to repatriate him because he was doing a scholarship for Cambridge University and our parents valued education and didn't

want to spoil that. My foster parents said, 'You're one of the family.' I'd been with them for four years. 'You can stay with us.'

My mother went back on her own, which must have been terrible for her, which is the poignant point in your play. The first time I saw it at the Cockpit Theatre that really hit home. I thought, 'My gosh, I wasn't the only one.' I didn't know of any other Kinder. Everybody told me, 'You're lucky that they were still alive.' So I felt really bad for not being thankful they were still alive.

I didn't want to go to Germany and I was forced to go because, when my mother came back without me, my father, who had with difficulty got a job as a judge in the court of Meinz, served a court order. He wasn't a total stranger like my mother because he had sent photographs from Shanghai. I knew what he looked like. I never thought he was dead, so I could relate to him. But we couldn't talk with each other.

My foster mother, who had said, 'You are one of the family,' had to take me to Germany and leave me there, which was a repeat of the Kindertransport original experience, but far worse. I felt so betrayed by my foster mother, by everyone. She said I was one of the family, but clearly I wasn't, because she had to ditch me.

My parents learned English. My father taught himself British law in Shanghai, passed the exams in order to get a job practising there, because it was a British protectorate. His English was too perfect. I used to challenge him that he talked like a textbook. But my mother learned English very quickly. I learned German very quickly when I was made to go there because I wanted to listen in and get the gist of what people were talking about. But I was so angry I deliberately muddled the grammar, which you can't undo. So I can speak German as fast as I can speak English but it's incorrect. It's intelligible but people have difficulty not laughing.

I think that my mother was the most damaged of the four of us. She never talked about her experience during the war. We couldn't talk with each other. I didn't want to listen. I didn't want to hear. I didn't want to ask questions. I just didn't want to be in Germany. I was repatriated against my will.

My parents were decent people. They realised it was a big mistake. I refused to do anything. I just ran out when things got too much. We were right down near Lake Constance in a little village. That's where my mother ended up. My parents couldn't live together because there was such a shortage of housing. My father had a tiny little rented room and there was nowhere for my mother. There was unimaginable chaos at the end of the war. I only saw the remains of the chaos four years after the war. I had the idea that if I ran and ran and ran, I would come to the coast and stow away on a boat and get back to England. But I just went in a circle and came back. I couldn't even get lost. At any rate, I think they realised pretty quickly that it was a big mistake and they let me go back to England.

The deal was that I would come out for school holidays, which I did and gradually got to know them. But it took almost a year to get back to England because I had no nationality and no passport. It was before nationality was given back to Jews and I wouldn't have wanted German nationality anyway. My foster mother couldn't enter me into her passport because I wasn't legally her child, so I had to have a travel document which was a large piece of paper with 'Person of No Nationality' written across the top.

I got back to England but nothing was quite the same. I completely lost my trust in people. But I had the animals on the farm. I could get the emotional sustenance from the animals, particularly the horses. I was mad on the horses. Horses are enormously comforting. They just nuzzle you and accept you just as you are, which is something that people have much more difficulty with.

The four of us... My brother Martin had the same problem... we could have a nice time together, we could talk about anything as long as no one mentioned the past. If you cut off a huge part of your experience as taboo, you can't have a relationship of any depth.

Martin actually chose to go to Germany. He met a German girl in Cambridge and they chose to settle in Germany. If you choose something you make it work. If you're forced to do something that is unbearable then it doesn't work.

Lil

'The real mother demanded the child back.
The foster mother faced her trial. Who will try the case,
on whom will the child be bestowed?'
The Singer in The Caucasian Chalk Circle *by Bertolt Brecht*

'Biology is the least of what makes someone a mother.'
Oprah Winfrey

My grandmother, who grew up in Liverpool and then lived in the Lancashire seaside town, Southport, was called Lily. I named Lil, the character in *Kindertransport*, after her because she was more or less of the same generation, perhaps a little younger than the character. I also wanted to acknowledge my own mother-line in the play, the northern background of my family, but set her home in Manchester to mark the difference from my own background, keep it separate. My own granny, a gentle and mild-mannered woman, slightly genteel, was very different to Lil. Growing up in Liverpool, I came across many working-class women, industrious and no-nonsense, devoted to their families in a non-sentimental way, who also ran a job alongside looking after their children. I see Lil as being an active member of her local church, which is how I imagine she heard about the Kindertransport and why she took in Eva in the first place, out of her Christian principles to help those in need. Essentially, she does this not out of any sense of duty but because she cares. Lil has a big heart. She also has her frailties and dark side, aspects that are less apparent but still significant.

Actress Eileen O'Brien, who played Lil in the 2007 Shared Experience production, also hails from Liverpool and grew up there in a large family until she went to Goldsmiths College in London to study Drama and Education in the 1960s.

Eileen has worked as an actor all her life except for the period when her daughter, Hannah, was growing up. Having a daughter has always helped her balance work and home life. She moved to Hebden Bridge in West Yorkshire when Hannah was born and has lived there ever since. Working with director Polly Teale on two productions with Shared Experience were, she says, highlights in her career so far. I spoke to her six years after the production, when Eileen had recently returned from Australia where she had been playing a role that brought the themes of *Kindertransport* into focus from another perspective.

> *Kindertransport* was special because it's a wonderful, quite disturbing play. This story was specifically about Jewish children and the war, and Polly (the director) wanted it to be much more about mothers and daughters. The relationships are difficult and unfulfilled and nothing is as it should be. It meant so much to the audiences we played to up and down the country.

> I have just looked at the play again and I'm thinking, 'God, I didn't play Lil right.' She should have been much tougher. I played her as being quite motherly and nice, which of course she is as well. She was a tough, northern mum. Like when she's putting Eva on the train to be evacuated: that's a bit harsh, when she's made the journey from Germany, to put her on a train again. Also in the attic with Evelyn when she tears up all the letters and photographs. I remember finding that really hard to bear at the time, and now I find it even harder to bear. I don't know why anybody would do it. I think she does it because Evelyn wants to do it. Evelyn wants to pretend that her past doesn't exist.

> I've just been doing a play in Australia, *Forget Me Not* by Tom Holloway, about the child immigrants who were taken from single mothers in this country and taken off to Australia and Canada. So it goes on a lot, doesn't it? All over the world, all the time, it seems, children are moved from one country to another. In this play I've just done, again I've been two ages, the Liverpudlian mum of the main role, Colin, who was taken away from her when he

was three and shipped off to Australia. Then, because he's such a mess of a human being, an alcoholic and so on, his daughter forces him to face up to his past and try to trace his mum. She says, because her mum has just died, 'If you want a relationship with me then you've got to face this.' So he does. It's also a play that goes back and forth in time. I think that about three thousand children went over to Australia up to 1970, so it was still going on quite recently. What's interesting is how difficult it is when the parent and the child meet, because the child's fantasy of the mother is so strong and how wonderful it's going to be when they're reunited, and also from the mother's point of view as well. Obviously the child is never forgotten. The child lives on in the mother's imagination as well, so when they meet it's nothing like either of them have ever imagined and they can't really cope with it. They haven't really got that much to talk about and they haven't got a relationship, basically. Their relationship is with a fantasy and what you want your child to be in your imagination. So I think that it's not surprising that Eva didn't want to take up with her mum when she comes to collect her and take her to America. But it's really hard to accept that she doesn't want to have any contact in later life, and wants to wipe out the past completely. Is that because she's Jewish? Or German?

I remember the fondness between Lil and Eva. I remember meeting her. It's quite fun. She makes her throw the label and Star of David away. It's like she's saying, 'I'll look after you. You don't need to be labelled. You don't have to be punished any more in this way. You don't have to suffer that indignity.' She sings to her. I remember going on the train and later in the house, the wardrobes and the train. It was quite a painful play to do. I'm always happy to leave plays behind once I finish them, and you say, 'Right, that's that.' And you move on. But I think it's a particularly painful play – putting children and babies on trains and having to stay behind as the parent. It seems so horrible and such a cruel thing to have to do. And I think the scene at the end where she's getting rid of the past like that. Looking back, I don't think that Lil is all that nice really. I think I wanted her to be nice. It would have been more productive to have repaired the damage between Faith and Evelyn, just be a bit cleverer about it really, rather than tearing up letters. She's never written as a clever woman. She's written as a woman with a good heart who's trying to do her best.

I would like to think that Lil might have let Eva choose if she'd known that Helga survived and came for her, and if she didn't want to go back then I'm sure Lil would have been happy to keep her.

It's a tough play. In a way, the pain carries on after the play finishes. It's so hard to throw things away that mean a lot. If the letters hadn't been burned, if all those memories hadn't been burned... if there had been some contact... Well, I suppose there's a feeling that Faith will carry on, but she hasn't got a lot to go on, has she?

It seems as if a lot changes for Lil, a hell of a lot. She goes from just being this quite tough working-class woman from Manchester who decides to do a good deed, for whatever reason, and then gets involved with this little girl who's from another world, and so Lil must have to adjust, because you feel as if Eva and Evelyn have accomplished more than Lil did in many ways. Just in worldly terms, I mean. You feel as if Eva's cleverer, and Evelyn's cleverer than Lil, maybe more successful financially and so on. You feel that Evelyn's living in a smarter house than Lil, that kind of level of success. There's a feeling of distance between them. Lil's closer to Eva as a little girl, and even to Faith. You don't feel as if much of Lil has rubbed off on Evelyn. I didn't ever feel that Evelyn felt like my daughter, as if Evelyn had moved away. It was a cool relationship. I imagine that they were in touch with each other and they would visit each other. I don't think I felt that Evelyn wouldn't welcome her.

A Christian family at that time would assume that everyone should be Christians and that's all there was to it. Not that they would force Jewish people to be Christian, but if a little girl was living with them in their house and the little girl said that she'd like to be baptised, they would see that as a good thing because everybody should be Christians. At that time, I'm talking about. It wouldn't be the same now. After the war there was a whole different mentality about other races and religions and so on. It was the way. And if it was a Christian family and somebody wanted to convert, people would just be pleased. They wouldn't say, 'What about your religion? What about your heritage?' Even now, if somebody said that they wanted to convert, who knows? But nowadays people would go to more trouble, if they are caring or intelligent at all, to respect people's own background, culture, heritage and religion, I'm sure they would. Lil also isn't that bright, is she? She's simple, down-to-earth, not very imaginative. She's doing a good thing, and she does it well. She's not in any way cruel to Eva. She gives her a good life. She loves her. Definitely.

Towards the end of Act Two, Evelyn says something about Lil being as bad as Hitler. There's this very bitter moment between them. Lil says, 'Am I Hitler? Did I start the war?' And Evelyn replies, 'You might as well have been.' But Lil is together enough to say, 'It doesn't matter what you say to me, I'm not going to go.' So there's something about that which suggests that she's heard this stuff before. Yes, I think that's how we played it. Because it would have been a completely different scene if Lil had thought she meant it. And I don't think that Lil would have coolly been able to then carry on as she does. There's a degree to which she sort of knows it's just Evelyn in a bad mood. She's not really winding Lil up. But it's terribly extreme stuff to say to somebody.

You do think of Lil as the rock. But by the end, I wonder if there's a letting-go that happens for her in some subtle way. Maybe there's a way in which she lets Evelyn grow up a bit. Maybe there's a way in which she 'babies' her slightly. A little separation occurs between them. Lil has protected Evelyn – maybe that protection is lifted a little.

Faith

'She's of a completely different generation and life experience.'
Actor Sarah Shanson on Faith

'Parents can only give good advice or put them on the right
paths, but the final forming of a person's character lies in their
own hands.' *Anne Frank*

'Sometimes the Second Generation describe it as this
"presence of an absence" if their parents didn't talk.'
Ruth Barnett, one of the Kinder

I chose the name Faith for Evelyn's daughter as I could imagine her choosing it for her child as a symbol of her relationship to Christianity: searching for a different source of strength other than her Jewish origins, her parents and what has gone before. Yet, in the Jewish world, such a turning away and baptising her child would be seen as a tragic loss, a betrayal and denial of where her true allegiance ought to lie, especially as the aim of the Nazi Final Solution was to eradicate Jews and Judaism. By converting and taking her daughter with her, Evelyn could be seen to be responding to this threat by doing the very thing that those who were persecuting her family and 'race' wanted to achieve. Yet in the name Faith lies hidden the quality of the original name I gave to Evelyn's daughter, Hope.

Faith, according to the Shorter Oxford English Dictionary means:

> Confidence, belief especially without evidence... Fidelity...
> A pledge, a solemn promise... the fulfillment of trust

Lily Bevan played the role of Faith in the Shared Experience production of 2007. She studied Social and Political Sciences at Jesus College, Cambridge, and Acting at RADA, and is Artistic Director of Osip Theatre and the London Collective. She has written, produced and directed at theatres including Trafalgar Studios, King's Head Theatre, Old Red Lion, Finborough, Latitude Festival and Playwrights Horizons, New York. As an actress, she has worked at the Donmar Warehouse and Wyndham's Theatre. She has also worked as a researcher for Alain de Botton's The School of Life, for writer/actress Emma Thompson and for *The Huffington Post* UK and USA.

At the time of the production, Lily was just turning twenty-seven, a few years older than the character of Faith. Six years on from the tour she found that, when she looked back at the script, she could still remember many of the lines.

> It was like hearing a song that you know, like a Beatles song, and I think it's because the characters have their own distinctive voices. It was my first or second job out of drama school and I had never been on a national tour. One of the reasons that the words of the play were so familiar was that wherever we were on this voyage it was like the world of the play was the ship, like such an anchor. I'd been to university and drama school by that point, and I'd been living away from home myself since I was eighteen, and was quite used to that. So whilst I could remember the experience that Faith's having of leaving home, I wasn't so nervous in the world myself or in a flimsy place emotionally, and when as an actor you're taking on heavy stuff you need to feel quite rooted in your own life.

> I loved the courage of Faith. There are so many parts for women that are flimsy or half-baked and the women don't seem like real women, and there are so many plays where there just aren't any female characters or they just carry trays around. Then you come across a play like this when you're a young actress and it's just like, 'Wow.' This character is brave and real and complicated and suffocated and then gets to speak and fights for something. She's loyal and messed up and all these things that women are brilliant at being.

It's lovely that all those women are related to each other, because there's an energy line through them of fear and grief, so we worked out that there was like a chorus of those feelings that we could draw on and echo from each other, and because we rehearsed together we were quite in tune with how the women of that family manifested those things and experienced them.

I felt deeply moved by the history, and very proud of my country for having initiated such an act. I was very close to my grandfather, George Bevan, who served heroically in the Second World War. He was working class, from Tooting, and began as an ordinary soldier then got promoted in the East Surrey Regiment and became a sergeant. They were an infantry regiment in the front line in the advance in the liberation of France, Belgium and Holland after D-Day. He was one of the first English soldiers to get to Berlin and Hitler's bunker. He was involved in the battles at Arnhem and his platoon was cut off and isolated behind the German lines. Many of the regiment were killed and he found himself in charge of a small group of soldiers who hid out in the countryside for some days, avoiding German patrols before they could get back to rejoin the Allied Army. He was mentioned in dispatches and given some kind of medal. I felt resonance with that when I read the play.

I was lucky enough during the tour to meet Kindertransport survivors, and I went to have tea with an amazing man called Zigi who ran a shoe factory and who had come over on the Kindertransport. He'd been sent to one of the very posh British boarding schools which had given him a full scholarship and he ended up being head boy. Then he started his own business and now he was a multimillionaire and he gave a large percentage of his salary back to the boarding school. He was the most patriotic person you've ever met and the most loyal to this school, and I just thought about that allegiance and sense of connection and that patriotism, but not from who you would expect. You think that those people who love posh boarding schools are like good old aristocratic types, but this was a young German boy actually. So that was just utterly what the play's about, being lived out by this lovely old man who came to see the play and invited me to tea. Talking to that man was like talking to my granddad about those things. You're lucky if you get to listen to stories like that. And for this play to be a way that those stories are shared and new stories come to be connected with it, is really something to be proud of.

With Faith there's a real sense of wanting everything to be okay, and getting it wrong all the time, of there being a problem. In that first scene, packing the boxes, there just seems a real heaviness around her mother and I felt really touched by that confusion. Your only guess as a child is that it's you and you're not really good enough or that you've let them down, or if only you could do something a bit better or say the right thing or make the right choice about your future. I can really relate to that. My parents had a hairy divorce and there were times when there was a great deal of pain around our family. When you're very young you don't have any facts to make any guesses, so you tend to think that you must have something to do with it. I think that Faith feels that.

She wants to leave, but she wants to leave with her mother's blessing, and knowing that her mother's going to be okay, and she doesn't feel that that's the case. She doesn't know why, but she's quite sure. It's not as if Faith is hopeless or afraid or a person who wants to live at home for ever because she hasn't got a clue. It didn't feel like that. It just felt like she needed to know.

I felt that she was at an interesting stage of life because there was still childish behaviour, loving her dolls, the train set and sitting there reading a storybook, but also she was about to leave. There was a sense of last chances: before you leave this house can you solve the mystery, because once you go, you know things are going to change fast. Something I like generally about work as an actor is: why is this day different from other days? What is happening today? For Faith, it's whether she can she get somewhere before she goes. Can she get some answers?

It's archetypal, isn't it, finding secrets in the attic, treasure in the cave, and all that kind of stuff. Finding lost letters is great. So of course you'd be interested in that. She just

thinks it's a German girl or a distant relation of some sort.
She doesn't know anything about the family at all. Even if it
were a great-aunt or something it would still have been
really interesting to her, and a revelation. I think she's
reading with a big vested interest but it's only later when
she starts to realise the truth.

It's interesting that she hasn't gone through the attic before.
Perhaps there's a sense that she's always wanted to open
every box in that house and never has, because the thing
that's prioritised is keeping the peace and keeping her mum
happy. She has a sense that it's not good to go poking
around, so she's always behaved herself. I remember the
time I lived in a house with a step-parent who I didn't get
on with. I had never had an emotional outburst for years,
decades, and the day I left for university I had a total
explosion, a full panic attack, hyperventilating, shouting,
out of control. It was because it was the day I was leaving.
That's a similarity, isn't it? Finally you can let loose. She
knows that there's an escape route, so if something terrible
does happen… and her granny Lil is around, you know, and
she's a safety net in a way.

Lil is so important. She's always comforting. She says to
Eva, 'I won't leave you. You can say what you like to me,
I'm not going to walk out of this room.' On some level,
that's what every child wants to hear from their parents, 'Be
as awful as you want, I'm not leaving you. There's nothing
you can say that will make me go.' Faith doesn't quite feel
like that. She can't rock the boat too much. So that's why
it's so cathartic when they do have it all out. Actually,
Evelyn does love her deeply and loyally, but they need to
say that to each other, and I'm not sure that Evelyn's been
able to say it.

There's a lot of unspoken stuff about the dad leaving. It's
one of those relationships where perhaps Faith is a bit of a
mother. I sensed that, rather than Evelyn looking out for
Faith in the divorce, it was the other way round: that Faith
was worried about the effect that the dad leaving had had
on her mother and was looking out for her a lot, which is
something that often happens. Not making a big song and
dance about it. Feeling responsible, thinking, 'This is hard
for me but I'll be okay. I'm not sure how Mum's going to

cope.' My mum left my dad and I felt terribly worried for everyone. I didn't really feel, 'How am I going to deal with this?' I felt, 'How am I going to help them deal with this?' I share that characteristic with Faith of being quite level-headed and then experiencing strange, volcanic surges of emotion.

We gave Faith's father a name – I think he was called John. He might have been an architect or some kind of chartered surveyor. He was kind of stable and we made the decision that perhaps he'd met someone else. They'd both tried to be quite civil about it, because Evelyn wouldn't have a huge, screaming row with him, but she'd shut herself away. I think we did an improvisation of him leaving, saying, 'Don't you want to talk about it more?' And she was just like, 'No. No.' It was like a crucible with a closed lid. It's mentioned in the play and it's another thing leading up to this day being different from other days. It's in the recent past and you have to acknowledge that he's left. And because it's a play about women, it doesn't mean that you don't have to ask questions about the men. I've been in plays about men, of which there are many, and it's important to ask questions about the women. Just because you don't have scripted characters, it doesn't mean that they're not important in the formation of the characters that we do meet.

Helga gets rejected by Evelyn, and Faith does too in that she's not getting the truth, not really getting the connection that she needs. Eva/Evelyn does this thing of standing at arm's length from both of them. Helga goes off on the boat. Faith goes off out of the house. There are all these women leaving to go on this journey, and it's important how they say goodbye to each other. In a way it's a play about that.

Faith has nothing to do with Eva. She watches her, but she never has a scene with her. They don't exist in the same reality. Eva's world moves about a lot. She's on the train and she's very active, always climbing around on top of everything, and the set was being used to tell stories about the spaces she was in, whereas my space as Faith was very claustrophobic. My job was to make my world closed, not open. So my attic was claustrophobic, and in order to get out of the house I'd have had to go all the way down, past

Lil and Evelyn. I wasn't alone and I wasn't in an open space. It's quite different if you're in a closed, musty space that's full of secrets than if you're out on a train. So Matti [playing Eva] and I had to work in the same space on the stage, but we had to inhabit totally different imaginary spaces and make sure that we didn't get in each other's way, though she would sometimes get quite close to me. But it was really important that she didn't touch me because that wouldn't have made any sense. That's why theatre's great now, because there would have been a time back in the day when we would have been on totally different parts of the stage, separated so that it was very clear, or with scene changes. It's so much more interesting to work in the same space, bringing together two different meanings and time periods, because you do affect each other, and these echoes are expressed in physical ways, such as when Eva runs past Faith and her hair blows a little from the speed of Eva's skipping.

That book is just terrifying. *Der Rattenfänger. Struwwelpeter.* The book I was reading from had pictures. The Ratcatcher was around a lot. He came very close to me. His breath. He was more like an unseen ghoul or a sense of something. I think that Faith is haunted by the fact that her mother's haunted by it. You can sense when someone you love and are close to is haunted, and that's there in Evelyn. All the stuff that Faith says at the end, about 'You hyperventilate when you see a traffic warden' or get the shakes when she sees a guard. Faith has worked out that this is not normal and it's not like she's schizophrenic or has depression. There are these specific things that happen to her when she's around authority. So she's very conscious that Evelyn's being strongly haunted by some kind of traumatic event. She's got that far.

After the confrontation scene between Faith and Evelyn at the end of Act One, I used to black out. I couldn't remember what had happened or where we'd been standing or anything. It would get so full on and I'd very often cry a lot as Faith. And that would make me short of breath. Evelyn was really, really strong... so when she got really strong with me I used to find it quite scary. It felt like she was such a volcano. There was a sense that I have to take care here, not because this poor woman is so frail, but because there's a crucible with a lid on. It's different.

When we rehearsed the scene where Faith knocks on the locked attic door at the beginning of Act Two, we did an improvisation that went on for much longer. I was just knocking and knocking to get the sense of really, really trying to get in, and to be feeling really rejected and remorseful for causing this flare-up and wanting to be loved, to be liked and not wanting to leave on a bad note. Locking yourself in a room is quite a powerful thing to do, because you've made a decision and the other person has no choice. So at that point, locking herself in the room didn't feel weak and vulnerable, it felt like another thing she was doing that was quite hurtful and difficult to deal with from Faith's point of view. And again that thing of 'I have to look after you. I have to manage this.'

Coming in and finding everything torn up was awful. Heartbreaking. Faith was feeling, 'I had just started to get my head round the idea that this was the treasure map to this stuff that we all need to work out together, and then before I've had a chance, you've destroyed it. It's so confusing and difficult to understand, so immature, to tear something up, to do it before we've talked about it.' I remember being really upset when I saw all the things torn up because we had real photographs, you know, copies of photographs. So they'd be there all torn up and Pandora [playing Helga] used to hand-write letters every single night which would be torn. That was important. So I had an attachment to them. And we'd done exercises where we'd all brought in treasured items to get that feeling of when stuff really matters. Just awful. I remember in the staging being quite on my own. Lil and Evelyn were together and I came in and it was all on the floor, then I was on the floor trying to put it back together, and I remember looking up and seeing them standing together at the side of the stage and suddenly feeling really exasperated and exhausted and quite on my own.

Faith changes the cult of silence that has fallen over that house. She won't close the boxes. She doesn't take no for an answer. I don't think that Lil wants her to either. I think that Lil is ready for this to come out. On some level she thinks that it would be better if everybody knew about this, because Lil knows that they can survive it. Lil's all about love and she's quite straightforward, and if you're there for everyone every single day and you make the sacrifices that she's made to look after Eva… to put food on the table, then that counts for something. Evelyn doesn't need to worry that her relationship with Lil is going to disintegrate all of a sudden, which I think she does worry about, because she doesn't tell her when her mum comes.

In the end, when Faith does go, she's got what she needed, which is that she feels her mum is going to be okay. Well, not necessarily okay, but that something has shifted. At least she knows, and there's a chance that they can talk again. It may be that Evelyn can never do it, but at least Faith's got the information now, and that's different.

I think Faith would go and look into Judaism. She may choose it, and it might have some real healing for her.

In the last four lines of the play, Evelyn says, 'Have you got everything you need now?' and Faith says, 'More or less.' So they're actually talking to each other about this. Then Evelyn says, 'All done in here then?' And Faith says, 'Yes we are.' 'More or less' isn't yes, but it's better than no. It's more about some things than she'd thought, less about some things than she had hoped. It's 'Yes we are' whereas at the beginning it's 'No we're not'.

Alexi Kaye Campbell as the Ratcatcher and Pandora Colin as Helga in the 2007 Shared Experience production © Donald Cooper/Photostage

The Ratcatcher

'The monsters of our childhood do not fade away, neither are they ever wholly monstrous.' *John le Carré*

' "War is like night." She said, "It covers everything." '
Elie Weisel

He came in a waking dream.

When I first read testimonies by Kinder about the journey across Europe to safety, I found myself imagining a train as it sped through the countryside. A figure suddenly appeared, dancing on the tracks as if leading the way. This figure was heading towards somewhere unknown. He resembled a depiction of the Pied Piper of Hamelin in an illustrated edition of the Robert Browning poem that I'd read as a child. I wondered what he might be called in German. I discovered Der Rattenfänger, the Ratcatcher, subject of a two-hundred-year-old Goethe poem that was set to music by Hugo Wolf. The Brothers Grimm also rendered their own take on the tale of the thirteenth-century vermin infestation of Hamelin and the haunting pipe player who rid the town of rats only to be cheated out of payment for his work. The manner of his revenge – emptying the town of its children – echoes some unknown historical event, perhaps the Children's Crusade, or mass deaths caused by a lethal epidemic. No one knows for sure what happened. Where history is hazy, myth takes shape. In my mind's eye he was at once a magical, alluring, enchanting figure, a liberator who promised the children adventures in a big wide world beyond the confines of home and family. Yet how much could he be trusted? Was his intent benign or malign? What danger might lurk at the end of the path he promised? Was there any coming back?

It was commonplace in the Germany in which the Kinder were raised for children to be told cautionary stories that were intentionally frightening and warned what horrors would befall if you did not behave yourself. In *Der Struwwelpeter* by Heinrich Hoffman, the 'Shock-headed Peter' of the title is an unkempt, wild child who is not to be tolerated. His graphic, lurid, yet strangely matter-of-fact illustrations depict characters such as Augustus, who won't eat his soup and consequently fades to nothing before dropping down dead after five days; Harriet, who plays with matches and is burned to a cinder; and Conrad, who sucks his thumbs only to have them cut off by the Scissor Man.

Eva's *Der Rattenfänger* book is not an actual book, but one that I fabricated, an amalgamation of these disturbing elements, a cautionary tale about what happens to all the other children too even if only one is naughty. Like a psychic policeman who sniffs the slightest whiff of something amiss, a dark cloud forms overhead, and when it descends it takes on seemingly human form that promises treats but is utterly implacable, ruthless and compels the helpless and awestruck youngsters into the abyss.

There is something eternally elusive about the shadowy forms that emerge from the unconscious. We may comprehend them a little but they defy logical interpretation, and provide clues rather than answers to what words can barely hope to express. The truth about the Ratcatcher is that he cannot ever be entirely understood. He is essentially mysterious. It is best to approach him, when interpreting his role in Eva's story, with a sense of imagination, and be open to a host of possibilities.

Only after visualising the figure on the tracks and developing his tale did I realise that the rat motif connects with the Nazi propaganda that often compared Jews to these vermin that had once brought a plague upon Europe. What does it do to a child to be labelled a rat? What does it do to a person to be cast as such an appalling pest that they must be exterminated?

What is brewing in the collective psyche of a culture that makes it project such fear and hatred onto another group of people? Fear can take an infinite number of forms, so the Ratcatcher may be as much death-camp victim surfacing to take revenge as a storm trooper hunting more prey. He can metamorphose into whatever is dreaded, whatever may lurk in the realm of the Shadow.

The Shadow is described by psychoanalyst Carl Jung as 'the thing a person has no wish to be'. For here, deep in the darkest recesses of the repressed unconscious, we bury what we cannot bear to face, what is most feared and abhorred about ourselves.

The Ratcatcher is Evelyn's own shadow, the darker side of herself that embodies her shame, pain, blame and grief, all the things she wants to disown and can't bear to face. He represents her unacknowledged fear of being taken off to some dark place (as much inside herself as out in the world), never to return. If he is the child-stealer who conjures naughty children away from their parents, then what is more wicked than committing the ultimate crime of rejecting her own mother? He is the Jew whom she betrayed and the Nazi whom she escaped. He is the mortal dread of being found out and punished. He is a shape-shifter who oh-so-readily slips into becoming all the people in uniforms who may send her away or bring down the forces of officialdom on her for being an alien.

He is the only man in the play because, in Evelyn's attic, in her psyche, she has a wounded and damaged relationship with her 'animus', the masculine part of herself. For her, the masculine is a danger and a threat. So wherever she encounters any man who may turn out not to be as ordinary as he seems, even if he is a Postman delivering a parcel or a Station Guard with information about the last train, she senses danger.

The role of the Ratcatcher in the 2007 Shared Experience production was played by actor and playwright Alexi Kaye

Campbell, who has worked with many companies including the RSC, the Royal Court, Chichester Festival Theatre, Manchester Royal Exchange and Shared Experience.

It was the most exhausting thing I have ever done in my life!

I remember feeling emotionally absolutely drained by the end of it. But obviously the rewards of that were that you knew that you were in something very special, and every night there were people who were absolutely gripped and riveted by the story and by the production, and you knew you were giving a profound experience to people.

Even though I loved the play when I read it, I remember being disappointed. I thought, this is a play with all these wonderful parts, but of all the parts on the page it seems to me that the Ratcatcher is the one who had the least to do. I need a part that is going to be fulfilling, which will give me enough to get my teeth into. The bits that were there… little bits… I mean, I could tell that they could be wonderfully done, but I didn't feel there was enough. Then Polly started to talk to me, and expressed her vision of the play. She had this sense that the Ratcatcher was going to have a much more significant presence. She really intended to make his presence, shall we say, a central motif, something very powerful, and to bring him out even more than he is in the text. Then, of course, she had me hooked. As it turned out, not only did I feel like an absolute, integral part of that play in the rehearsal, but I've never worked as hard. I didn't feel as if I was ever on the sidelines.

We started working through improvisation and physicalisation. We started exploring the psychology and the whole subconscious world. Of course, it is a story in which subconscious plays a very, very big part because ultimately it's about denial, and wherever there's denial there's also an incredibly rich inner life which is desperate to come out.

There's a very dark heart to *Kindertransport* and a great sadness in it. What naturally evolved, and what is already implicit, is that the Ratcatcher came to signify that dark heart of the play. He signified the dark heart of everything that is repressed and feared, but also came to signify the evil that we do to each other and the dark side of humanity, which is very much connected to that period of history. It's very much about lost innocence and childhood, a kind of stilted childhood, of a child wrenched from its parents. And the Ratcatcher is very much connected to a childish imagination and childhood fears. So we were able in that production to bring all that very vividly to life.

There were a lot of exercises around physicalising self-hatred, things that we're frightened of. They were very abstract exercises. Then slowly this kind of creature started to evolve, which was this abstract... I don't know how to describe him... he was this sort of... presence... a darkness. I remember when I was working on the play I had a little sketchbook, and I was doing pictures of how I visualised the Ratcatcher and a lot of the pictures looked very much like things that you would be frightened of in a children's book. I was always aware that this presence was seen through the eyes of a child. I remember thinking all the things that I was frightened of as a child, like the Child Catcher in *Chitty Chitty Bang Bang*. He had this quality of movement which was quite serpent-like, a creature that moved in ways which were very, very disturbing because it wasn't direct movement. It was all very reptilian.

There's a scene before he's mentioned, which must be about ten pages long... the first scene of the play. I was on stage from the minute the lights went up. I wasn't hiding, but I was wearing this blanket thing which covered me. I had my head turned upstage so that when the lights went on I was in a visible place but sort of camouflaged. The scene started and then ten pages into it the Ratcatcher is mentioned and slowly, to very haunting music, my head started turning and I suddenly appeared. Pretty much every night I would hear gasps in the audience. What was extraordinary was that nobody had noticed me until I moved, and that was fantastic.

I wasn't on stage for the entire play. I had quick costume changes, for instance. I had to go off as one character, come on as another. I was on stage for a very good deal of it, probably three quarters of it at least. I do remember feeling incredibly connected to the play and I carried it around with me for quite a long time. It was very dark. Very dark. In the last week of the run I had this terrible nightmare, a night terror. And I put my hand through a window and cut myself very badly. It was all very dramatic. When you look at it you think, 'Well, was it the play? Was it?'

Most of the time my performance was very non-verbal, and I found that it opened up a different part of your mind, which is connected to the subconscious. Developing my first movements I remember visualising terrible things I had read and seen about the Holocaust to find what the Ratcatcher had to represent... and one of the things he represents is the evil people do to each other. I read two or three books about the Holocaust, and of course I knew about it and had read books before, but you're doing it with a very different part of your brain because you're entering that world in a kind of imaginary way. We watched documentaries, the Academy Award-winning documentary *Into the Arms of Strangers* about the Kindertransport. We had a Holocaust survivor come to talk to us. I went to university in America and one of my professors was Elie Wiesel, an amazing man. When I was in his class we'd studied his book *Night* – devastating, but brilliant. I remember reading *Night* again. I hadn't read it for about fifteen years. I remember reading details. And images. And you're not reading it academically or to learn, you're reading it to enter that world with your imagination, with your soul, and it takes you to very, very dark places. And you knew that you had to go there because the play demanded it. So I remember drawing on that energy and in that first scene, when I'd move and see Eva for the first time and play with her, I'd always try to have these thoughts in my head of these terrible things, because I knew that I had to embody that. So you're going to be carrying that in you. It's not about the movement itself, it's about what the movement represents, and you have to do that wholeheartedly.

The costume looked very much like somebody you'd see on a street – not so much in London, but in New York you see vagrant characters who are covered in blankets and you don't really see their body under the blanket, so it's this indiscernible sort of shape. And I think this was right in a way because it captured that sense of this creature that was amorphous and could take on different disguises. The way we played with it, the Ratcatcher kept appearing. Like the scene at the train station – suddenly he'd appear with a suitcase. He kept changing form. He was very chameleon-like in that way. The costume was black, very dark, slightly amorphous, like a blanket over me.

When I became the other different characters, there'd be no sense of the Ratcatcher. They were like cameos, snapshots of ordinary people, but I was always aware that they had a greater significance, especially with the same actor playing them. They become this kind of Everyman seen through the eyes of Eva, and seem to be foreign or intimidating to her even though they might not be so in themselves. The Postman's not necessarily a sinister character. I remember there's a sinister quality to the Border Official, when she's had her pockets emptied on the train. There's an undercurrent of violence there which was disturbing to watch and to play, this grown man treating this little girl in a way which is psychologically very violent. I remember thinking that there was something even more disturbing about the fact that one minute he's rifling through her pockets and then he's giving her a sweet. It's like those people who can be kind one minute and awful the next, and can behave in a very unconscious way.

I don't want to call it a 'woman's play' because it's not. It's much more than a 'woman's play', but it is a story of these women whose lives are shaped by historical events and circumstances which have been pretty much entirely created by men. It just happens to be women at the heart of it, which is refreshing because most plays aren't. And the only men we see in the play – every man we see, I think, is in a uniform. They're all in an official role. So there's a sense of these women who are trying to live their lives, trying to know themselves, trying to move forwards, but the realities and conditions of their lives have been set out by men in uniform a lot of the time. It obviously works having the same actor. There's this male figure, and the male figure… I don't know if this was intentional… is, for the most part… dark.

The fact that all the characters in the play are somehow seen through Evelyn's eyes gives it this weird kaleidoscopic quality and also makes the play very much about childhood too. When we're children we do feel that we're the centre of the world and we see characters not perhaps as they are but through that prism of childhood, and when we grow up we learn, some of us, to be more objective. You see the characters through her eyes, and realise that it's about that aspect of childhood that she can't get out of. She's a woman who's frozen, because when Evelyn grows up she's frozen, so she's like a child. She's stopped, in denial. That's very, very powerful and it's why the ending of the play is so devastating.

The Ratcatcher's journey mirrors Evelyn's journey. The more Evelyn feels fear, the stronger he becomes. The more she's in denial, the more his presence is inflated. He's like a mirror image. To some extent she does to her child, to Faith, what has been done to her. She felt rejected and abandoned, even though we know that's not the case. And she rejects and abandons a part of Faith by being dishonest. So it's interesting, that kind of through-line, that repeat of behaviour.

There was a moment right at the end, the moment of rejection between Helga and Eva when she doesn't go on the ship. Throughout that last bit I was on stage but very still, downstage right, literally not moving, with my head bowed. Then right at the end Evelyn's left on stage on her own with me and I looked up at her and she stared at me and I remember the last gesture was this collapse of my head. It was something about facing the truth. Telling the truth defeated the Ratcatcher. Look him in the eye and his power goes. I think it was hopeful. It's interesting, it depends what one means by a happy ending or a hopeful ending. When a character comes to know something more about themselves than they did at the beginning of the play, is more honest, then this is a hopeful ending. It's about honesty. Knowing thyself. She knows herself better at the end of the play.

Paul Lancaster as the Ratcatcher, Gabrielle Dempsey as Eva and Emma Deegan as Helga in the 2013/14 Hall and Childs touring production © Robert Day

Two Directors

'Every director works differently.' *Cate Blanchett*

'The work of a director can be summed up in two words.
Why and How.' *Peter Brook*

'There is a different kind of vulnerability when a
woman is directing.' *Jane Campion*

Each different director's take reveals new angles, highlights
unexpected aspects of the play, sometimes subtly, sometimes
strikingly. There are two directors, both of them women,
with whom I have worked closely, nearly fifteen years apart,
on their own distinctive productions of *Kindertransport*.

Abigail Morris was founder and Artistic Director of the
award-winning Trouble and Strife Theatre Company before
she became Artistic Director of Soho Theatre Company
(STC) for fifteen years. There she directed many new plays
and, in the early days when she was newly appointed, played
a crucial role in bringing *Kindertransport* to the stage for the
first time. She saw its potential and programmed it for production when it won the Verity Bargate Award. Abigail's
detailed dramaturgical input, alongside Literary Manager
Jack Bradley, was invaluable in refining the play for the stage,
and her perceptive, attuned directing enabled it to make the
mark that it did at the Cockpit Theatre in 1993. Not long
after that production, I was visiting a friend and met Polly
Teale, at the time a freelance director, who told me that she
too would love to direct the play. Polly has created a unique
body of work as a director and writer, including a trilogy of
plays inspired by the Brontës, and the award-winning *After*

Mrs Rochester. Nearly a decade and a half after that initial conversation, Polly did direct *Kindertransport* and brought the distinctive, physically expressive style of Shared Experience theatre company, of which she is Artistic Director, to bear with powerful results.

Nearly twenty years after Abigail's first production and six years after Polly's revival, each was ready to share the essence of their very particular perspectives on the play, personal connections with its themes and how they each brought alive their vision for the stage.

Abigail Morris

I met Abigail in the autumn of 2012, around the corner from the Jewish Museum in London where she had recently become Chief Executive. She at once made the connection between being a mother and being a director – she had given birth to the first of her three daughters after first directing the play. Recently, she had been invited to give a talk about *Kindertransport* in a local secondary school, and was inspired to share the experience with her youngest daughter.

> I asked if they'd seen it, and they hadn't. I really believe in plays being living. Then I thought, 'Well, my youngest child is eight and that's obviously how old Eva is.' So I thought, 'Why don't I bring her in.' I tried it out in the kitchen and she read it absolutely perfectly straight off. We went in, just read the first scene. It was incredibly powerful. The students completely got it. They asked really good questions. Getting them to first base was quite interesting. Like, what's going on? What's actually going on? – Faith's trying to leave home. When Evelyn gives her the box of glasses, what's she doing? – When she says, 'Have a box of glasses,' she's also saying, 'Don't you dare leave.'
>
> For me, what's interesting is that obviously I've done the play so many times, and I did it before I was a mum, and

then after I was a mum, so that my understanding of those relationships became really different.

I think it's the most fantastic play, unbelievably brilliant, because in those early scenes it has that total simplicity. It reads so beautifully. It's completely clear, and you don't need to do any pyrotechnics. It is just what it is. And yet it is so multilayered. Someone said something to me about it being naturalistic. It's not at all naturalistic. But because it was so simple and felt so human, to them it felt like a domestic drama, which of course it isn't. It's about separation, and about identity. For me, it was the Eva and Helga thing. It's really in my head as a mother, that line, 'You are my jewels. We old ones invest our future in you.' And, 'Being there.' That's what it's about, being there. It had an incredible effect on me.

It was quite a risk when we put it on because nobody else seemed at all interested in it. And then, of course, it was this massive hit. And people were queuing around the block. It became absolutely huge. And people staying in their seats just sobbing. The effect was phenomenal. Then we did it again in New York [at the Manhattan Theatre Club]. Then at the Palace Theatre, Watford. I loved the space, that attic, in New York. When we did it there we did a performance for survivors, for Kinder. And one of the things about the New York cast was that they were very emotional. They kept crying all the time, and I kept saying, 'You have to not cry. You have to let the audience cry. If you feel like crying then don't, because then the audience will cry. But if you cry then you'll do their crying and they won't have to cry. It's much more moving when you don't.' I had to try to give them lessons about the stiff upper lip. Anyway, after the performance, when they came out, there was total silence for about a minute. It was one of those performances when the hairs on the back of your neck are standing on end. There were a few questions, and then one woman stood up, and said, 'It's really wrong, this play. I am seventy-five and I lost my mother sixty-five years ago when she put me on the train, and I still look for her every day, on every street, every time I'm looking at a bus stop or people are getting off a bus, or every time I'm in a train station I look for my mum. There's no way I wouldn't have gone with her if she had survived. It's just so wrong, the idea that someone wouldn't go with their mum, when it's my dream.' I was so overwhelmed by this old, old lady who was still looking for her mum every minute of every day, and then telling me that the play was wrong. And I thought, 'How can I respond to that?' Such grief that she was carrying around. And there was this pause. Then this man stood up and he said, 'I have to say that my mother survived and I didn't go with her.' It was a really chilling moment.

When we did it at Soho, I remember saying, 'People won't come on a Friday night [the start of the Jewish Shabbat or Sabbath] because it's mainly a Jewish audience. We shouldn't have higher ticket prices.' We used to have higher prices on Friday and Saturday. I said, 'We need to attract a wider audience.' And it was completely packed on Friday night, with Jews, because of course there are loads of Jews who don't want to do traditional Shabbat but wanted to do something Jewish. I really want Judaism to continue and I don't want it just to be the very right wing. I want there to be a living religion. I think that's one of the things that's lovely about *Kindertransport*. It enables people to connect to their Judaism.

What's so amazing is that it's such a specific story and yet… for example, a friend of mine brought a man who was splitting up with his wife, and he wasn't Jewish, but just the fact that he was having to leave his children, he was howling at the end. It really deeply connected with people about separation. I remember so many occasions of people who were so moved at the end of it.

I remember doing a workshop with a group of kids and they thought Eva was right and Helga was wrong to send her away. As a mum the preservation of the life of your child is so important. Your love for them is so strong that you can't realise how much they love you. Helga was probably right to send her away but I really hate that Evelyn doesn't go with her. I find that so painful. That idea that you'd cling onto life… I can imagine that totally… that you'd cling onto life just to see your child again. I remember at Watford I'd just had the baby, she was only a few months old, I was still breastfeeding, and I would drive back, it was a long way, just to feed her, then come back in the evening. You can't really understand what it's like to love a child like that until you've had one. Also, that Helga was alive when her grandchild was born but never knew her, I find unbearable. I really believe in choosing life and that survival. So she was a very strong woman. She lived a long time.

The thing that was hard was getting the Ratcatcher right. The image that I wanted was this great big shadow right across the stage, and actually physically that was really hard to do. We best got that in New York, but even then you needed more space. Some of the decisions I made as a director have been put into the script, like the Nazi Border Official drawing the Star of David on Eva's suitcase. I really like the idea of the attic. I suppose that's the whole, slightly Freudian thing, the unconscious and the hidden, and it being 'away' in the house, upstairs. The actress who played Lil in the first production was quite old but she practically had to crawl under the stage to get up the stairs. It was important for me that you came *up* into the attic. There were lots of boxes. Basically there was a very white set with a dark window, and the Ratcatcher sat in the window playing and watching. The idea was that he would do all the announcements. He was the person who would literally take her. So he read the announcements for Osnabrück and all of that. We also played that amazing recording by Richard Dimbleby, the Bergen-Belsen report, out of the same place, and Lil and Eva looked through this dark window as if at the film flickering. And he kept changing. All he'd do was put on a hat for the Postman, or an armband for the Nazi. The key thing about the Ratcatcher is that he needs to be really quite nice, not just be the evil character. I always felt that the Guard is trying to be fair and the Postman is trying to be jolly, but just happens to be behaving in a really viciously anti-Semitic way without intending it.

In the first production we tried to base the music on the song 'Runaway Train'. I was keen to move it away from sentimental cello, Jewish music, which was the obvious way to go. The Ratcatcher played all the incidental music on a little penny whistle. It wasn't a play that needed huge amounts of music. The music was in the language, I think.

I just wanted to make it as simple as possible. So Eva and Helga were just there and this old standard lamp that was in the attic was their light, very localised. Then Evelyn and Faith came in and the lights went on, and Eva and Helga were still there, and they just walked round them and didn't see them. That idea of what have you got in your attic, what are the skeletons of your past that you might not see?

I was insistent that Eva was going to be a child. It was really, really important to me that you see the child and really feel that vulnerability. In a way, she'd have to do far less acting. It was that thing of being really simple. It needed a child who would just do it, who would just go, 'Why can't you protect me?' and when her mum gets cross with her, suddenly go, 'Will you miss me?' thinking, gosh you might not even love me. All the kids could pick up the German very easily and do the German accent – the characters only spoke in a German accent when they were speaking English with a German accent, but when they were speaking German to each other they didn't have a German accent. That was really important. They were talking to each other in their own tongue. It needed to be someone just prepubescent so that she could look like a nine-year-old, but then put on some high-heeled shoes and look sixteen or seventeen and do that scene at the end as a young woman.

Evelyn is a really difficult part to play. Each actor wants her to be sympathetic, but that scene with Lil, ripping the letters, they found really hard. And the actors needed to know what they were ripping up. We spent quite a lot of time on that, even though the photos just looked like bits of paper to the audience. It's important to appreciate how Evelyn destroys everything and Faith has nothing left.

Lil is really warm, like the person you'd always want to be, that you'd feel so comfortable with. What's interesting about Lil is that you don't have much of a sense of what she's like. She is the mother figure. She exists as the fantasy of your mother, who exists especially for you. There isn't really a sense of Mr Miller. She's there, she picks her up, and yet she is really limited. She should have thought before taking her to the newsreel. It mattered how Lil buttoned up her coat near the end when she came up and said, 'I'm just going out.' The way she did up her coat, being cosy and yet quite strong, quite fearsome in her own way. You wouldn't mess with her. She'd be a lioness. She'd protect her brood.

Faith still needs to have that youngness of wanting to be independent, of being an adolescent trying to separate but not being able to, being a child and not a child.

There's this perfect production that I've never quite been able to achieve. Somehow I wanted the train to be taken out of the box and then it lights up – that thing of the miniature becoming the big. The other thing that I was very keen on was that there would never be a scene change, it just went seamlessly, so Eva just stood up and was there and it just flowed.

It's like music. It really connects with that inner child that's in us all. And that fear. But it's interesting now, because when I did that little reading of it in the summer, this summer, for those kids, I suddenly thought, 'Yes, I'm a mother and I could be Helga and I have got this child who's Eva's age. But I'm almost going to be Evelyn with a child leaving home, and actually I'm finding being a mother of adolescent daughters very, very challenging. Whereas before I just thought that Evelyn is horrible to Faith and Faith's so messed up; now I'm much more sympathetic.

It was always a very difficult play to direct because it brought up stuff for actors. Every play brings its own stuff with it. The play comes with baggage. It's interesting that when you go to a counsellor, they say, 'Let's unpack that.' when you've said something. And that's such a great metaphor for the play, that suitcase. You're unpacking.

Polly Teale

Whilst preparing to direct a new play – psychological drama and ghost story *Bracken Moor* written by Alexi Kaye Campbell (who played the Ratcatcher in her production of *Kindertransport* seven years earlier) – Polly, who has a daughter, tuned in again to the dark emotional explorations that marked her approach.

We have this central character who, because she's experienced this trauma in her early life, has constructed a life in order to make herself feel safe and secure, and that's very understandable. Something as terrifying and traumatic as having to leave everything that you know, and the knowledge that you would have been killed had you stayed where you were, the fact that everything that gave her security was ripped away, has meant that she needs things to be absolutely certain the whole time. There's something very powerful here. Obviously, it's an extreme example of how we as human beings, in order to protect ourselves, can create lives that ultimately become self-destructive because it becomes a kind of prison, that certainty, almost impregnable. In Evelyn's case, there are all these defence mechanisms or ways of putting on armour, but there's a brittleness so that ultimately she is unable really to live and to grow, be intimate with other people, all the things that make life worth living – these things become impossible. I think it's wonderful the way that this is explored in the play, and the way that the metaphor of the attic with everything, all of her past, packed away, is gradually exploded and she's pushed to the point where she has to open up that wound and look at all the stuff that she's been trying to hide. This is something that every single one of us can relate to. Although it is a very extreme version of it, that idea that everything we think we're doing to protect ourselves actually ends up sabotaging our life is a very powerful one.

I love the way the play uses that story and imagery of the Ratcatcher and the notion of a nightmare presence. That is very interesting physically. I had a sense that there was something there that could be explored and manifest in some way. In theatre you can make things visible that are usually hidden inside us. So all that interior world of emotion and imagination, memory, all the stuff that's locked up, the opportunity to excavate that part that's been buried and lost. In Evelyn's case, her need for safety has been so absolute that she has made this inaccessible even to herself. So that metaphor of the Ratcatcher, this figure from childhood who's so terrifying that you can't go near, is a really powerful one. Of course, theatre allows you to have those two layers of reality at the same time, so you can see that this is a woman in her fifties who has lived in some ways a very comfortable life that's allowed her to construct an existence that you could say has functioned fairly effectively. But at another level, she's a little child who's absolutely terrified that any minute now she's going to be annihilated by this creature. There's something really exciting about a play like *Kindertransport* where the writer is able to find a way of making that not just visible, but actually palpable.

I'm always interested in characters who feel very complicated psychologically, and particularly characters, I suppose, where there's a part of them that's so buried that it's almost inaccessible and yet it's actually dictating everything, every choice that they make.

I suppose I can identify with Evelyn. And clearly her experience is very extreme, but most of us have stuff in our history that means that we're protecting ourselves in some way. Of course, one relates to the characters too. The terrible dilemma of her mother Helga in that first scene… Any parent trying to imagine themselves into that very particular situation, it's nightmarishly frightening. And throughout history parents have had to make those choices. Even living in relatively peaceful, relatively prosperous twenty-first-century Britain, still the impulse of the parent to protect their child… that's the thing that parents struggle with all the time, that protective instinct and the fact that that's not always the healthiest one.

I'm from the north of England, from Sheffield. Actually, I don't know if this is relevant, but when I was ten I went to Auschwitz. We were in Poland, not with my family, with a group of young people, with the Woodcraft Folk [a movement for children and young people]. We were there for about a month, and it was all organised for us, and part of what we did was going to visit Auschwitz. At the age of ten. And watched all the films. It's interesting now because you think that probably no organisation would dare to take a ten-year-old to Auschwitz without their parents. I don't have a regret about it, actually. I must have known a bit before I went, not very much. I knew about the war and maybe a little about who Hitler was. I was incredibly

shocked and rather haunted by it. Certainly made it very
vivid, rather than something that happened in history. I can
remember those heaps of shoes and piles of things that had
been taken from people as they arrived, odd things like
artificial limbs. I think, though, that I would have
responded to the play regardless of that, because the play
explores in a very profound way the idea that our adult self
is often a reaction to things that have happened during
childhood and that seems to me to be very, very rich
territory.

How easy it is to forget that all of the war generation were
so deeply affected and yet, at the time, there was very little
recognition or opportunity to explore or understand or talk
about it even. Basically you put your best foot forward and
you didn't complain. You were lucky to be alive. And now,
you think they went through this hugely traumatic
experience. I mean, men would be away for four or five
years and they'd come back and their children wouldn't
even recognise their own father and feel completely as
though some stranger had come home and taken their
mother away from them. At that time there was no
opportunity even to think about why you might be feeling
like that. You just had to shut it all away, which is very like
what Eva has to do. So, I suppose what's interesting about
Lil is that she doesn't have a sophisticated sense of what
Eva's going through. She doesn't have the language to talk
about it psychologically, but she has a sort of instinct
somehow for... that love, that place of love where she's
coming from. There's something very moving about that
little girl, on her own, becoming completely attached to her.
It's always incredibly moving, the fact that human beings
have that capacity to do that. The capacity of human beings
to do the most terrible things to each other, and on the
other hand human beings can go way beyond. You see that
Evelyn has been deeply damaged by this experience, and at
least she managed to go on. I suppose that Lil, with her
love, is in large part responsible for that.

It's so interesting that thing of the next generation and how
they carry that weight of something that has never been
talked about and yet you absolutely know that there's
something going on, the energy of that trauma is present in

your life in a very palpable way and yet you're not given the opportunity to understand. I think that's one of the great things about the play, it really is a sort of rallying cry almost. Again, Evelyn's trying to protect Faith. She doesn't want her to have to know these terrible things. She's also trying to protect herself because she's afraid of what will happen if she talks about it. And so often that instinct to try to control things turns out to be destructive. We watch Faith gradually explode that, gradually take bigger and bigger risks until she's saying, 'We can't carry on living like this. You have to tell me about this.' I think it's often true that the next generation, our children, will inevitably bring us up against that part of ourselves that's brittle, and they will kick against it and expose the things that we're trying to hide. That's very recognisable in many parent/child relationships.

On the one hand the play is set somewhere very, very specific, in the attic of a house. You know that there are certain things you have to have in it. In the script, you know there's got to be a tea set, a case that has all sorts of dolls and games. There's also an opportunity to create a metaphorical attic, that's about this locked room inside Evelyn.

There does come a point when Evelyn actually locks herself up there and Lil has to kind of 'break the door down'. Everything works as metaphor. It manifests itself physically which is what theatre is all about, bringing something from the invisible into the visible. That metaphor of being locked up in that room is such a powerful one. With Faith there's a kind of refusal to accept the block and a need to open something up that's very painful.

One of the things we chose to do was to have a line of four or five wardrobes, which is slightly odd, but it's possible that you could have five wardrobes tucked away in the attic. There was something about things shut away, rooms within rooms. We used the wardrobes as doors within the story. At one point the wardrobes were used as a train. They were both something real and they could transform into something else. Immediately there's something a bit surreal about this. It's not quite any old attic. On the one hand you want to make it a very real, believable place. You want to believe in the house that's underneath it, believe in the life that is being lived in that house and that this woman has put things up there that for whatever reason she hasn't wanted to keep downstairs, but she hasn't thrown away. It's almost like her whole life is in that attic, layers of time and things that go right back to Eva, to the part of herself that she's trying to bury. Yet she's not actually thrown those things away – they're still there. That's a choice in itself, because she could have destroyed them. You have to find the things that are in that room and make them completely believable, and at the same time you want the space to be entirely suggestive and open to being turned into somewhere and something else.

So you start the play in Eva's bedroom, her being read a story… the packing before she goes away to England… and that's intercut with the scene however many years later when Evelyn and her daughter go up to the attic in order to look for stuff for Faith to take away to university. Then you suddenly find yourself with Eva at the station the next day and Eva is leaving. So you go from a very interior scene to this moment, obviously a very key and traumatic moment in the story, when the train pulls out of the station. This is huge and resonates throughout the whole of the rest of the story. You go from a very interior, naturalistic scene – although the Ratcatcher was in the background in our production – to a moment when you conjure it up as if you are inside Eva's skin and Helga's. It has to feel like the train is almost like a monster. You want to create the subjective experience of being taken away. A room full of a strange jumble of stuff can quite easily transform. Certainly these wardrobes worked very well. The slamming doors were very like those old-fashioned trains. One minute it can be that, and the next minute it's turned into something else. The best sets do that. They just sit there being whatever they were when you first saw them, they keep flickering and changing. That sense of transformation is what makes it interesting.

You should feel like everything that Eva does, that's Evelyn too. In rehearsal, Marion Bailey, who played Evelyn, played all of Eva's scenes at some point because I felt it was really important that she had the experience of being that child and internalising all of that. There's something exciting about the idea of a part of you that's split off from yourself that is still completely present. The actor's task, the one playing the adult Evelyn, is to make sure that that little girl is inside her, and everything that happens to Eva is not just in her memory but in her body. There's always the challenge of really believing that they [Evelyn and Eva] are the same person. I remember doing quite a lot of improvs [drama improvisations]. I remember one where they were both swans, and one was a mother swan and the other was a baby swan, and swans are... on the one hand there's this poise and elegance, but there's also a capacity for real violence. Trying to do exercises as the same animal, to help the actresses feel like they were the same person. We looked at finding little mannerisms, particularly the 'tics' and 'tells' around anxiety. We explored them both having the same little gesture that they made. So it was very physical.

With Shared Experience, one of the things that we try to do in rehearsal is explore physically the inner lives of the characters, all the stuff they're trying to keep hidden. There's an exercise where I clap my hands in the middle of a scene and the actor has to physically express whatever it is that they are feeling in that split second. In reality it may be that two people are sitting drinking tea, opposite one another, but when I clap my hands one person might be wanting to kill the other and the other might be really terrified and want to crawl under the table. So it's a chance physically to explore emotional states. Then, when I clap my hands again, you have to return to the scene, sitting, drinking tea. When you return to the 'real' scene, of course, the energy of what's just happened is still present. So, although you might just be drinking tea, the way you stir your sugar or the way that you are fiddling with your ring... there's a tension in the body that remains, and informs and affects what's happening on the surface. With a play like *Kindertransport* that is so useful because much of what's happening is subtextual.

I remember spending quite a long session exploring the notion of poverty and destitution, and the idea that that is not really far away. We explored everybody being like rats, and hunger, of what could happen to you if you don't escape, even right through to death. We also worked with our own personal experiences. Most actors have had experiences of not knowing where the next bit of money's coming from. Also looking at what it's like to be part of a group that's demonised and made to feel like it's subhuman. You're exploring a state of being, notions of shame and humiliation, loss, fear and anger.

In the case of the Ratcatcher, we moved away from the imagery in the storybooks, of somebody with a Pied Piper fairy-story look about them, to somebody who got at the essence of what it might mean to be considered to be scarcely human, somebody that you might walk past in the street, living in a cardboard box, whose clothes have become completely filthy. We wanted him to be an embodiment of all Eva's worst fears of what could happen to her, almost like an embodiment of the Holocaust. He was on stage right at the beginning, so that when they come into the attic, there's something there in the shadows. Probably at first you might not even notice it and then gradually you become aware that there's somebody crawling out from the wardrobe. He was on stage for quite a lot of the production, the sense that for Evelyn, and for Eva, he's always there, never far away. What you're doing, scene by scene, is exploring what does that presence mean in this particular moment and why does he suddenly emerge here, why has the writer chosen to bring him to life here? Then, saying that we're not just going to have him here but see him gradually emerge during the course of the scene gives you a chance to investigate that tension in the play. We worked with these huge overcoats. Originally there was something more like a cloak. Then it was something like a vagrant but taken as far as it could go to the point where his clothes were literally about to disintegrate off him. Then we bound Alexi's hands and feet in rags and we looked at lots of images of people in the ghetto trying to survive when they had absolutely nothing in the very cold weather. Looking at what happens to a human being when they are taken to that place as a result of becoming scarcely human. So it evolved a lot during the rehearsal period. It came out of the research. That's always a challenge when you do that kind of work because it means that things can change.

The lighting was very important because you want to help the audience to understand where you are. So when Eva went from the bedroom to the station, the lighting went from a relatively cosy glow to very stark… I think there was a bit of green in it… how a railway station might feel at night with the lights they use in order to say stop and go. It was very atmospheric.

You could say that Hitler, the Nazis in Germany at that time were predominantly men. We start the play with the mother and daughter together and then the child is taken away. All of those figures that the Ratcatcher plays, the inspector on the train, the man at the railway station, the Postman, are not necessarily baddies. It is interesting that Helga is alone with her child on that evening. Eva's father wasn't there, and it's very believable that he wouldn't have been there because in some way it would have been seen to be the mother's task to prepare the child for going away. It doesn't mean that he wouldn't have been equally concerned. It certainly was a society in which gender roles were very defined. Eva has two mother figures in the play and you don't have a father figure. You kind of feel as though, growing up as Hitler was coming to power, your idea of what masculinity might be capable of, in a sense it's the antithesis of the archetype of the mother. Faith says to Evelyn that any time she sees a man in a uniform she goes into a panic, and there's no doubt that the seminal experiences from our childhood colour every experience we have later, whenever we meet anyone who somehow reminds us of that early experience. So if when you're a child there are lots of men walking around wearing swastikas on their arms and they're the prime force behind that movement, it would affect your sense of men and what men are capable of, wouldn't it?

Kindertransport looks at the cultural, political and social landscape and how this impacts on an individual at the most private and personal level. How does that affect the way we feel about ourselves and see other people and the choices we make in our lives? The relationship between those two things, the bigger picture and the interior lives, feels to me like a very interesting relationship. I suppose that you could ask what effect anti-Semitism has on the way somebody feels about themselves deep inside. Then, in turn, who they become in the world and how they affect the bigger picture, the relationship between those two things.

Music

'And to his lips again
Laid his long pipe of smooth straight cane;
And ere he blew three notes (such sweet
Soft notes as yet musician's cunning
Never gave the enraptured air)…'
Robert Browning, 'The Pied Piper of Hamelin'

Directors and students often ask where they can find the 'Ratcatcher Music' that is mentioned as the very first stage direction at the top of Act One, Scene One, and then recurs throughout the play. Their guess is as good as mine. This stage direction is an invitation to imagine. There is no particular traditional or specially composed melody that I have ever had in mind. Each production requires its maker to discover their own Ratcatcher Music for themselves.

For the Shared Experience production in 2007, Peter Salem took on the task of creating a score to accompany this expressionistic, physical rendition of the play. Peter has worked extensively as a composer for the National Theatre, RSC and many regional companies, as well as writing the music and creating the sound for a number of Shared Experience's productions which, in addition to *Kindertransport*, have included *Anna Karenina*, *Mill on the Floss* and *War and Peace*. He now principally writes music for TV dramas and documentaries, and has composed a ballet score for the Scottish Ballet.

> We looked through the play in the beginning, spotting places where there might be sound, just very general ideas. Using a pipe would take it in a folksy direction, like the Pied Piper of Hamelin kind of thing, which I wanted to avoid. It would have made it more fairytale-like and tapped into a cliché, something people already feel they know. Obviously the idea of the Pied Piper of Hamelin is there,

but we wanted to take it and twist it. The Ratcatcher should feel more dangerous. Even though the Pied Piper leading children away and them disappearing is a horrible idea, there is somehow that sort of sweetness with folk tales. We wanted to get the edginess. It is interesting how these horrendous tales do get 'twee-ified'. Maybe that makes them even more grotesque.

The script talks about the 'Ratcatcher Music', so it's obviously a critical way into the play. There's the mention of the mouth organ, which is important to Eva because she sneaks it out of Germany. It's a connection back to her Jewish roots and background to some degree, and yet it's also something that lures her away from it as well. It seemed like an interesting instrument to use for the Ratcatcher because it ties in a bit with the idea of the Ratcatcher as a kind of vagrant, and isn't connected too closely with the Pied Piper of Hamelin. I didn't like the idea of him being too Jewish as I don't think he's particularly to do with her Jewishness. He's something that takes her away. She's scared of ending up in this abyss by following him. The Ratcatcher is also a part of her psyche, so it should connect with her, and she's got this mouth organ that is significant to her... and it's something she actually rejects later on because Evelyn sees the mouth organ and doesn't even remember it when she's older. It was a very good instrument because I could use it rhythmically to mix in with train sounds and the idea of travel. So the Ratcatcher became not only a figure playing a mouth organ but also trains and boats and things that take you away, drawing you away from your past, your faith, your family, mothers from daughters... It can be connected in with that as well.

I wanted the music not to be too Jewish, but Jewish at times. As a folk instrument, the mouth organ is quite good from that point of view because you can get that slightly oriental feel from the instrument. The music that the Ratcatcher plays can sometimes be a mirror to Eva's Jewishness or show her past and origins, but mostly he's associated with leading her off somewhere, and that's what she seems to fear all the time, losing everything. It's ironic that in trying to avoid being led off she does end up losing her family and faith.

I bought several mouth organs. I'd never played a mouth organ in my life before, so it was a real journey of exploration. It's a fantastic instrument. The actor playing the Ratcatcher didn't play the music, it was all recorded. The music is a kind of mesmeric, strange melodic thing on the mouth organ which entrances you away. There's also the idea of building up multilayered sounds of mouth organs to create rhythmic pulsing sounds for trains and things. A lot of the music has an element of mouth organ, with some strains of Jewish music for memories of childhood.

Right at the beginning, there were some very slight underscores [music playing underneath dialogue or dramatic action in order to emphasise, heighten or contrast the mood] where there's a motif for Eva's background and home, and that's played over a clunking train sound, because, of course, the train is an important image, not only for evacuation but for journeys to death camps. It's very subtle. You probably wouldn't even notice it. For instance, when Eva and Helga are packing and talking about Eva leaving. Then at the train station there's a big number with quite a few mouth organs playing simultaneously.

What makes it filmic sometimes is combining the music with the sound effects, and that isn't done very often. One becomes part of the other. So you've got the train sound and the mouth organ is mixing in with that and working with it – the combination of those things creates a sort of landscape of sound rather than just a tune. People call it sound design. I do both. I don't see the dividing line. I think sound design is putting your speakers in the right place, and then mixing the sound in the studio, setting the levels, the technical stuff. I always do all the sound effects, and for me it's critical because they must work with the music and they have to be psychological, they can't be literal. They've got to be used like music. They're often non-naturalistic. It could be as simple as giving the train sound a certain characteristic, filtering it or adding some spoken words to make it feel not like, basically, you're hearing just a train in a station. Recently, I wrote a piece of music where somebody was sitting in a car with some windscreen wipers going and when I wrote the music I just knew that the sound designers would put over it this whacking, great, literal sound effect of somebody's windscreen wipers. So the music's trying to take you into the head of the person sitting in the car and the sound design is making you listen to the outside of the car's windscreen wipers. That's why I like to have control over the sound effects in theatre, because I think that they can work really well. You can blur sound effects and music into each other, like when you're using sea sounds or train sounds or boat horns, so that they each become part of music. This is needed in order to have the right psychological impact.

With the journey Eva takes, there is the Ratcatcher leading them into the station, so there is quite a strong Ratcatcher theme for being taken away. Then there's a train whistle. Then you get the mouth organs on the top with the train rhythm beneath. Then when she's on the train it settles down to a background rhythm with the repeated pattern in the mouth organs – that underscores the dialogue. You have to avoid interfering with the dialogue at that point, but still maintain a sense of the journey. So obviously when you're underscoring dialogue you thin things out and pull the levels down, but you're maintaining a sound. When you have silence in theatre it's often quite a shock because theatre is very, very quiet, and having a tone in the background just keeps things from being dead. If you have a piece of music and you suddenly lose it then it's a very different feel. So it's quite good, if you want to maintain the sense of her leaving, to keep something very simple in the background.

There are quite a few bits of underscore. The Ratcatcher would appear in scenes where it wasn't actually written in the script, moments where he would just need marking. Also, using sound in the most heightened places where emotional things are happening, a sense of her carrying something of her past with her. She had the bracelet and the watch in her shoe. So there was also a very, very simple theme which was just a jangly bell sound over a drone which would waft in every now and then when it seemed appropriate.

The stuff between Faith and Evelyn is much more prosaic and down-to-earth. It's contemporary. They're sorting out their lives, having rows and discovering things. Obviously when Faith's discovering stuff through the Ratcatcher book, there's sound there. But not when they're actually confronting each other. Although, towards the end of the play, there was some sound with the Ratcatcher coming in, this undercurrent when they have their final confrontation. There was music when there's Faith and Evelyn and Helga and Eva... it's all happening.

As well as harmonicas, I used string instruments, because I play the violin, but the way we used them was not orchestral, more tonal. Samples. Keyboard synths and electronic stuff. For the darker passages, like the Belsen bit with the projector, underneath that there are electronic sounds and distorted sounds as well.

There are several things that music can do. It can either heighten what's going on, or it can counterpoint the action, showing something which isn't there. In this production the Ratcatcher was often counterpointing, so you'd be running something under a scene which was connecting to the past. At the beginning there's an underlying menace; even though Helga and Eva are trying to keep quite positive, there's this feeling that there's something dangerous about the situation, something more than is in the script, although it's obviously hinted at. Quite a lot of it is about heightening, apart from those moments where you get the idea of the Ratcatcher or the past bubbling under the surface.

I love the fact that the quality of sound in a theatre is so significant. You can do things with very quiet sounds and very loud sounds, which you just can't do on TV. In some ways, theatre is more problematic because it doesn't quite embrace music in the same way that film does, but then film and TV can embrace it in some ways that you wish they didn't, overuse it, make it too sentimental. It's important in theatre to focus on the key moments. The whole atmosphere, the live event, sound and the way that you can change the space. So much is suggested, and so much is in the imagination, and that's why I love the combination of sound effects and music, because you can make pictures much more with the sound, which you can't do at all in film because it's all there on the screen. There's a great deal of suggestion that you can use, because you're creating boats and trains and journeys and streets and places in people's heads, musically as well as literally. The best steam train I made was actually with my cappuccino machine.

Kindertransport is fantastically evocative, such a psychological play, so there's plenty of scope for sound, and memory. Music is sometimes a short cut if you refer to sounds that you've used earlier for people or places. It's very important to make the sound world very consistent. Often, having a theme that connects a character to a place and using that as a recurring device is very effective.

Emotionally, music can take you somewhere, and often at that level it is just a question of suggesting, making a reference. Because the theatre space is so quiet, if you want to create certain degrees of tension, for example, then just adding a sound into the space can do that very well. There is an emotional range. With the Ratcatcher theme, you can get a feeling of anguish, desperation, separation, which you couldn't do with an actor squealing away, going, 'Oh, God, I'm feeling this or feeling that.' Just by adding in the music or sound you can communicate what a character is feeling. That's when the counterpoint thing works. Somehow music triggers the audience's capacity for imagination, so it takes you onto a different level. It gets you onto a different psychological plane. You feel you're being taken somewhere else. What I like to use it for in theatre is focusing-in on the action. So it's not like something that's plastered on the top. It's not distracting. And often a very quiet sound can focus you in on the actors, and then, when you take it away, leaving silence, it focuses you even more. And you wouldn't particularly notice that it's doing that.

I went into a lot of rehearsals, and I tried a few things out. It's become much easier now to get a score up and running in the rehearsal room, with computers, because you might have things overlapping. For example, in the train sequence there's two or three music cues that have to overlap. And you might want to hit a certain moment in the action and you have to cue that moment, but you might have something else that's still running underneath. So you build something that's running on different layers. Theatre is never fixed until the last minute, so you always have to be flexible, and that makes you write differently from the way you would for a film, where each sequence is 'locked' once completed. You have to be prepared to have a piece of material, then shift to another one, then shift to another one. The actual timing of those shifts could change right up to the opening night, so that has to be programmed in to how you're working.

I like to be as precise as possible because the difference between a note coming in at one moment and coming in at another is so significant. If you can make things absolutely coincide then that makes a huge difference. In theatre, I like having these layered music cues where you do one thing and then make a change. For example, one of the cues could be adding in a drone, or bringing in one note from an instrument at a certain moment – this is critical and can really shift things. It's the combination of the action and the sound that has an effect.

Design and Costumes

'A producer has to know all about everything from
set-building to costumes to acting.' *Alan Ladd*

'When I sit alone in a theatre and gaze into the dark space of
its empty stage, I'm frequently seized by fear that this time
I won't manage to penetrate it, and I always hope that this
fear will never desert me. Without an unending search for the
key to the secret of creativity, there is no creation. It's
necessary always to begin again.' *Josef Svoboda*

No matter how many times a play has been performed before,
a new production is a leap into the unknown. Each director
must discover the work as if it has just been written, search
afresh for their own distinctive theatrical vocabulary, con-
ventions and emphasis, whilst remaining true to the essence
of the play. A significant part of this process is finding the
design to house the world in which the vision can be fully
realised.

Andrew Hall was born in Manchester of a Mancunian father
and Scouse mother. He grew up in Surrey and started working backstage part time at his local theatre. After leaving
school he worked full time in production management, working his way up through just about every technical position
including flyman, ASM, DSM, stage manager, company
manager and assistant director. He won a place at LAMDA,
graduated in the late 1970s and has worked extensively in theatre, TV and film both as an actor and as a director. In 2008,
he moved into producing in partnership with Tracey Childs.
After together mounting a successful UK tour of Alan Ayck-
bourn's *Haunting Julia*, they came upon *Kindertransport*.

Andrew had been reasonably well informed about the rise of
National Socialism in 1930s Germany and knew what

Kristallnacht meant, but knew nothing about the Kindertransport before he discovered the play.

> This was a revelation. It grabbed me straight away, mainly
> because I couldn't stop weeping when I was reading it. It is
> clearly a very moving story, a very moving piece of theatre.
> What then made me even keener to do it was the fact that it
> combines both intense realism, what is going on in that attic
> room between that mother and daughter as their
> relationship reaches a crisis, and then a very theatrical
> experience in terms of how we negotiate the transitions to
> the memory of the past. I had seen *God of Carnage* [by
> Yasmina Reza] in Southampton in a production that Juliet
> designed and I liked that very much indeed. We met, we
> had a conversation and away we went. So that was the
> beginning.

Juliet Shillingford is a practising theatre designer with over
twenty-five years' experience. She has worked with a variety
of companies from the high-profile Curve Theatre Leicester
to New Perspectives, a company that takes quality theatre
productions to small communities. In 2007, her design for
The School for Wives was chosen as one of only fifteen designs
to represent the UK at the Prague Quadrennial exhibition of
scenography. This, together with her design for *Don Quixote*,
then formed part of the Collaborators: UK Design for Performance exhibition at the V&A. She lives in South London
with her partner who teaches set-building and drawing, and
their three children. She also teaches and runs theatre design
workshops at the V&A.

Juliet, like Andrew, had also not heard about the Kindertransport.

> Lots of people I've spoken to had the same reaction,
> 'What? Ten thousand children? I can't believe that
> happened and I don't know anything about it.' Often the
> delight of this work is that you come across things that
> open up a whole new world of study which is really
> interesting. So I came with no background at all. When I
> read it I found it incredibly moving. I found pictures at the
> Holocaust Museum in London of those children and I

practically can't bear looking at them, some of those tiny children that look so lost and so small. You think it's such an amazing thing that they came all this way by themselves. You're moved as a parent, because you can't help but put yourself into that position and think of your own children.

Then I watched a documentary, which was made maybe fifteen or twenty years ago, in which they took people back on the train to relive the experience. I recognised this woman who was a colleague of my mother's. She was in tears and finding the whole experience really difficult and her husband was comforting her. I never knew anything about this, and I don't think my mother did either. A lot of people don't talk about that period of their lives yet it's there in their background. When I first read the play I thought, 'Could this woman have really kept that secret for all that long?' Then I discovered about someone I knew who had never mentioned it. It's curious, isn't it?

Four months before the opening of a nationwide UK tour of *Kindertransport* for 2013/14, Andrew and Juliet had already met two or three times to discuss the design and were very much immersed in the process of integrating an evolving artistic vision with practicalities. They were still feeling their way into the overall shape and specific detail of things, throwing around ideas and giving them form. Initial research and preparations had already been undertaken separately a while earlier.

ANDREW. In preparing to direct *Kindertransport*, it became clear that the details of the historical events are, in a way, a backdrop. The heart of the play is the relationship between mothers and daughters and the pain of separation. It is about damaged people passing on that damage through the generations, the corrosive power of guilt and the destructive power of secrets and lies. These are universal and timeless themes, given particular force and focus by anchoring them in the obscenity of the Holocaust.

It has been very helpful to hear stories of the experience of Kinder to confirm that the experience of Eva/Evelyn is by no means unusual or far-fetched. The filmed interviews on the website of JCORE [the Jewish Council for Racial Equality] have been particularly helpful, and the extensive online resources of the AJR [Association of Jewish Refugees] have also been invaluable.

Knowledge of the logistics of the journeys of Kinder has been important in making decisions about the design of the set. In order to ensure that the fluidity of the writing, as it slides from past to present, is properly respected, we need to take the audience into different worlds in the blink of an eye. Clunking, time-consuming set changes are out of the question. Sound is also a potent tool in achieving this.

Interestingly, the other historical element in the play is that it is set in the 1980s. The '60s, '70s and '80s were decades in which the position of women in UK society changed radically, and these changes impacted on the relationship between mothers and daughters, not least in the marked change in their opportunities, ambitions and expectations. Faith's options are very different to those that were open to her mother.

JULIET. As far as research is concerned I look at things and read the text over and over again – sometimes a word or phrase becomes really important. We loved the 'chasm' and 'abyss' images. I looked at pictures of rocks and people jumping over gaps in the ground, like the floor at the Tate [in 2007, Tate Modern in London exhibited a temporary art installation created by Colombian artist Doris Salcedo, which took the form of a long crack in the floor of the Turbine Hall gallery space]. This gave me the idea of the raised floor, everything a bit precarious.

I also watched the film *Into the Arms of Strangers* [Mark Jonathan Harris' 2000 documentary about the Kindertransport].

I took lots of pictures in the attic of my brother's big Edwardian house.

I collected other pictures from the internet of houses, and looked at roof construction on building sites near my home. I liked how they appeared so enclosed and prison-like or cage-like with the interlocking rafters.

I also went a few times to Deptford Market – a great market for atmosphere, mostly house clearance, so full of old photographs and a jumble of possessions sometimes heartbreakingly getting destroyed by the rain while people buy old electrical goods that don't work. I will go there to look for old dolls and things for the set.

A friend recently found some amazing photographs of a European Jewish family from before the war there, very wealthy looking. She has rescued them and had them framed.

Other than that I draw on my memories, my childhood – how people dressed – how I dressed – the attic at my grandparents' house.

I try to imagine people like the characters, people I might know or strangers. I stare at people on the Tube and embarrass my children.

ANDREW. In our very first conversation, the one thing I insisted on was establishing the anchor point for the production as the play's 'present day' in the 1980s.

JULIET. The other thing was that the door, the entrance, was only to be used by the 'real' people, and that the other people had to come on and off stage in some other way so that they didn't use the same entrance as the 'real' people. They inhabit a different world and so they don't come through the door that's got a lock and a handle and everything that's real. But that real door exists. I always find that what you start from is what's essential. A door is essential, for the reason that it anchors the reality. Don't put anything on the stage unless it's really necessary.

ANDREW. I think the other word we used was 'permeability'. The set had to be permeable to memory in precisely the same way that the past leaks into the present, like when Lil turns her head and has gone from some time in the 1980s to 1939. So we have to have the theatrical language to be able to achieve that.

JULIET. Then at the second meeting I brought a model. I didn't really expect it to be so finished. It just suddenly appeared. The first set was a realistic attic with rafters and beams. It was quite rigid and everything was very much at right angles. We've moved on from there – we deconstructed that model, because both of us said 'What if...', looking at how roofs are made, and the beams and the rafters and wooden structure, thinking that was like the skeleton of the space. We talked about opening it up, opening up the angles.

ANDREW. I had recently done two plays that were incredibly realistic in the setting. For both of them it was very important that we were actually in the room. So when I saw this vision that both achieved the room and also had it floating in space, and with all the permeability and so on that we'd spoken about, I felt, 'Oh wow, now I know what it is possible to do.' Which is a huge thing. You can be much more imaginative in approaching the play precisely because that set has arrived and offered those possibilities.

JULIET. Evelyn's attic is neat and tidy – it shouldn't be messy. Everything must have its place. So if the angles of the set become too unreal, somehow distorting the symmetry, then that isn't right, because she's quite held-together and organised. It might be that in her head everything is falling apart, but everything needs to look like it's not falling apart, because on the surface it's not. It's her space. It's her world. So yes, taking from her, which I think I often do with a design. I think about who owns the space. You start from the character and whose space it is. We talked about her character, bordering on OCD [Obsessive Compulsive Disorder], but holding things together and it all going on underneath. We imagined that it's a recent thing that everything's fallen apart in her life, and so on the surface it still looks fine to everybody else, all her suburban neighbours. You don't want to walk in and the set looks wacky and crazy and at odd angles.

ANDREW. With all the plays I've recently directed, there's a wonderful expression, 'People leading lives of quiet desperation.' That's very appropriate about Evelyn. The idea of somebody just hanging on by their fingernails. The feeling that if they give an inch it will all fall apart. That's an important element. So that attic has its place. Everything is in its place, and of course Faith disrupts that by finding and discovering the train set and the dolls and all those things.

JULIET. We've raised the set off the floor on these beams because this adds to the slightly precarious feeling of her life – this order and this attic, I didn't feel that it was solid. So I didn't want the underneath, the floor, to be solid. We have talked about floorboards so the floor has some slits in it and light or smoke could come up through these. Then that raised possibilities that one end of the set is more realistic with the door in it, and the other end has this raised area with beams that can possibly become the station platform, or the quayside. Because it's just that little bit elevated, it gives the feeling of being on the quayside saying goodbye to somebody, or we talked about the scene with the Postman, with him walking around, as if she's standing on a step outside the front door. Those levels suddenly give you possibilities for staging those little scenes, which are the memory scenes.

ANDREW. We're talking about placing gauzes on the rafters at the back…

JULIET.…for shadows…

ANDREW.…which means that if you light it from the front it appears solid. If you light from the back, you have the opportunity to make it much more transparent. And you can project onto it so it becomes a potential canvas.

JULIET. For the Ratcatcher, possibly projecting shadows onto the roof so that he becomes a looming presence.

ANDREW. You also have the opportunity to build into that a few areas that are not actually gauze at all, they're made of stretched pieces of lycra so you can literally slip through. So somebody can suddenly appear in the space and, by turning the audience's attention one way, suddenly there's a figure standing there, and they have no idea how that person arrived in the space. Across the front, depending on the way that you paint and light it, you can suddenly have a railway line that you haven't seen before with people waiting on the platform and the last train has arrived into Manchester and her parents aren't on it. At the side, for example, you just need a little suggestion of water from a gobo [lighting stencil shape] and the sound of ships' horns and you're standing on a quayside for the departure of Helga. With the Postman's arrival, if Eva is tightrope-walking along the edge of the set, as if she was on a garden wall, then you can play that scene like that. So the set is incredibly flexible and achieves everything that I could possibly need to do. Then you add into that mix the lighting and the opportunities to use both the interior light within that space... and there are windows, dormer windows. So you have the opportunity for daylight.

JULIET. People can look out.

ANDREW. At the beginning, in that first scene with Eva and Helga, I really want a very strong sense of external threat, and that is achieved both by light coming through that window and also, crucially, the soundtrack. So we might combine the Ratcatcher theme with distant sounds of breaking glass, of mobs on the street, and perhaps at a key moment in that early scene you just hear a single shot, or something from far off, to reinforce the idea of an external imminent threat within that world... Then suddenly the door opens and we're in a domestic interior in the 1980s, and we don't understand that connection at first.

The other thing about the raised floor is the possibilities it opens up for the Ratcatcher, because on the page we have his shadow. One of the options we've discussed is that our Ratcatcher is a figure who appears within this room in a whole different reality again. So he's not in the present day, he's not in the memory, he's in the imagination...

JULIET. He's in the fantasy world.

ANDREW. We're talking about having a slightly oversized waste-paper basket in the set, as Helga and Eva are reading that story, then suddenly a pair of hands and arms and a head can appear out of it. Because we'll have travelling understudies [extra actors also on tour to step in and cover if any of the main actors are indisposed], we can have two, if not three Ratcatchers, so one disappears and one reappears elsewhere on the set instantaneously, in order to bring that idea of all-pervading threat engulfing the people within that space.

JULIET. It's the childhood thing as well, of being frightened of what's under your bed, frightened of what's in your wardrobe, and making him be that kind of figure who just appears out of familiar settings but it's scary because it's dark.

ANDREW. We've been talking about where we can utilise items that are actually in the attic that can suddenly surprise us. One of the things we've been toying with is having an old wardrobe with a mirror on the front placed upstage, and then for the arrival of the Border Official on the train, suddenly, like with the gauze, you light it the other way round and there's somebody standing at the window, then that door slides across and he steps into the carriage of the train. So we can take ourselves into that train with something that is incredibly simple, a sliding door and a window, but when you then combine that again with your soundtrack and lighting and everything else, you can be in that train and in that confined space in which Eva is suddenly in danger. It's little things like that which are so exciting, and so much fun because you go, 'Oh right, this is not just an actor opening a door and saying "Good morning, I've come home, darling."' There's so much more that you can do.

JULIET. It's the unexpected things, isn't it?

ANDREW. You have to be able, with this piece, to go from intensely real, complex, subtle, sensitive emotions and then suddenly you have the opportunity to show them in a way that makes them sit up. I'm not talking about masses of smoke drifting across the stage and spotlights shining. It's how, by choosing just to rarify some of the elements, it becomes theatrical.

Model box by Juliet Shillingford for the 2013/14 Hall and Childs touring production

JULIET. When people look at the design and at the set-up at the beginning and think, 'Oh, I know where this is going. I know what's going to happen.' It's making people be surprised by what they're seeing.

ANDREW. Allowing those two worlds to bleed into each other is the key thing.

JULIET. We've got the shape and in a couple of days we're having a 'White Card' meeting where you're talking about the physical size of the set and everything. We hope we're on the right lines in terms of budget. It will be costed from that point of view and people will go, 'Yes, that's great' or 'No, we can't afford it. Get rid of half of it.' So then from that I will develop colours and finishes and all that kind of thing. So we're at the stage now of doing that in a week or so, and then going on to costumes. We've rushed through a bit because of the deadlines imposed by our set-builders. So we suddenly had a flurry of working.

ANDREW. One starts with this blank sheet of paper. Then you have ideas, but that idea has got to come in under budget and survive twelve, sixteen, twenty weeks of touring. It's got to go from Southend, which is the size of a shoebox, to Milton Keynes, which is the size of a football field. So then it becomes about how you take that vision and make it buildable, transportable and affordable.

JULIET. It's a collaborative process, like with the set-builder and they come along and go, 'Why don't we make this out of whatever?' And you go, 'Oh yes, I didn't think of that, it's a really good idea.' You can take all those different elements on board and they become part of the whole thing. As you go through, things change. It's important to know when to make those compromises and when to say, 'No, I don't want to do that.'

ANDREW. It's that mixture of imagination and brutal reality in terms of what you can actually do.

JULIET. We've talked a little bit about costume so far. We haven't talked about there being any great distinction

[between 'now' and 'then']. I'm shying away from the
idea of it being colour and black-and-white.

ANDREW. The costumes are realistic with one exception –
the Ratcatcher. We also spoke about somehow finding an
element in what he wears that bleeds into the Border
Official, the English Organiser, the Postman and Station
Guard, so that we get just a hint of something that
threads through just as we'll get a hint in the musical
theme that will accompany them.

JULIET. I like it to be a collaboration. I never like imposing
a costume on an actor. It's really important for it to be
a dialogue and to have a starting point which is a
drawing or a bit of research which you'll show them
and say, 'This is where my head's at, but I'll come back
in a week's time and find out where your head's at and
see where we coincide.' I learnt early on in my career
that you don't just hand somebody something and say,
'This is what you're going to wear.' It makes the actor
feel that they've got no control or say, so their process
is totally separate from your process. It shouldn't be
like that. You're treating them like a mannequin who's
just going to wear what you've designed and not
treating them like somebody who's going through a
process of their own. I do costume designs but I don't
want things to be finished before people turn up. We
have limited budgets and rehearsal time so we have to
make a lot of decisions before the actors are involved,
and you hope that you can leave some of the decisions
for when the whole team of people are together. There
are things like what people do with their hair and what
shoes they're wearing.

ANDREW. We've spoken about wigs. The transition for
Helga, and how you show that somebody's the same
person but so radically transformed by their experience.

JULIET. Early on, you think about the problem areas where
it might suddenly hit us that we need extra money. Wigs
are a notorious area for this. They're expensive, and you
need somebody on a tour who can look after them. We
had discussions about Helga and how that
transformation might happen. Then recently I found a

reference to somebody wearing a headscarf. So we said 'Yes, let's go for a headscarf.'

ANDREW. That actually becomes a much more effective way of telling that story because somebody who we've seen earlier with luxuriant hair, the affluent woman we meet at the very beginning, is transformed into somebody with thin, damaged, unkempt hair. Then if you actually put a headscarf over the top of it, there are all of those memories that we don't know that we have of the images in the rubble of Hamburg or wherever it might be, because people always wore headscarves because their hair was filthy and there was no opportunity to wash it.

JULIET. When the headscarf idea came up it was as if we needn't have had all the conversations about wigs, but you need to go through all that process.

ANDREW. Precisely, having those constrictions makes your imagination work harder. It's the classic thing, you buy a three-year-old child a wonderful toy car for their birthday and they'll play with the box because their imagination enables it to be so much more. One very helpful line of dialogue in the script is 'This coat is going to have to last.' The coat's too big for the child. And if you put a big coat on somebody, they immediately look small, slightly lost within the coat.

JULIET. We only talked about one change really – Eva's transition from little girl to teenager.

ANDREW. The actor could be fifty years old, but what's important is whether they can bring alive the essence of being eight. It might not matter so much what they're wearing. It might come down to how they sit or how they touch their face. That's your way in. Realistically, you've also got to find the places where we can have a costume change – this is not necessarily going to be easy. As we read through, the key change for us was for Eva going from nine to fifteen, from young to the newsreel scene. When you then go to the seventeen-year-old, different again.

JULIET. A lot of that will come from meeting the actor, looking at their physicality.

ANDREW. On the first day of rehearsal, you unveil the set
and then, having started from that point, you can create
a working process and atmosphere in which the play
then takes shape, because all of this is preparation.
What we're doing now is building to the point where we
can enable the actors to construct together the reality of
the play and bring alive its emotional journey.

Janet Dibley as Evelyn and Gabrielle Dempsey as Eva in the 2013/14 Hall and Childs touring production © Robert Day

Creative and Essay Writing

'First I write one sentence: then I write another. That's how I write. But I have a feeling writing ought to be like running through a field.' *Lytton Strachey*

'Writing, to me, is simply thinking through my fingers.' *Isaac Asimov*

Most days, I take half an hour to practise writing freely.

I put on some music, usually contemporary jazz, or a Baroque classic, maybe Bach, and I write without stopping, paying no mind to grammar, punctuation or spelling, caring nothing about whether it means anything or makes sense. I dive into the slipstream, find flow and let the current carry me. I write on blank sheets of discarded A4 paper, used on the other side, from the scrap pile. I write with a pen not a keyboard. In this outpouring I am uncensored, liberated and, most importantly, the unconscious finds voice, surfacing like a waking dream into conscious space. All creativity involves a messy stage. All writing starts out raw, like vegetables plucked from the earth, muddy and misshapen before they are washed, trimmed and cut, then carefully prepared into a dish that might be served to others.

I travel to many different parts of the country giving talks about *Kindertransport* and also running workshops. I encourage students to let go and write imaginatively about the characters or specific key moments in the play, releasing a splurge that enables them to voice freely the images, flashes of feeling, sensations, hunches, impulses, half-formed thoughts and perceptions that the play is evoking.

One approach is to jot down as many words and phrases as possible for a specific area to be explored. For example, if I now choose a character name and write whatever it inspires no matter how strange, foolish or odd it may seem, I get the following:

> Evelyn – aloof, attic, glass, chipped, cigarettes, ash, waste, packing, closed, locked, blue, mask, divorced, alone, hope, determined, faith, resources, hiding, hidden, silver, containing, tight, clenched, wanting, ice, forget, regret, close, unopened, tearing, fragments, careful, clean, home, house, cope, crystal, swan, nest, refusal, panic, control, remains, smoke, sensible, senseless, shadow, safe, protect, pack, unpack, tea chest, silence, key, teapot, roof, sharp…

It is always worth writing beyond the point when it seems that you're finished – then more surprising and unexpectedly revealing words may emerge. So keep going. It is fine to write nonsense. Diving into the imagination is an illogical and chaotic business. There is no pressure to be right, simply to write.

Then, begin with the name of the character and collage as many of the words together as possible, connecting them with words of your own choosing to create a piece of 'raw' writing. Do not think as you write. Keep it moving. If you get stuck, write the name of the character again or any of the words. Play with the possibilities like a toddler plays inventively with whatever is lying around.

From these 'Evelyn' words, I create the following spontaneous piece:

> Evelyn is chipped at the rim, feeling sore and yet sensible enough to dig out a packet or more of the old cigarettes left stale in the wardrobe. She smokes herself senseless until she is ash on a blue day like this. Fragments of tomorrow sharp as ice lodge in the rafters and picking them out like splinters of hope is what remains. If she has forgotten to remember then she does not realise any more. Close the door. The key is in the packing cases behind the swan's nest. No eggs left in there now. Sometimes the panic comes. Does it hide in the silver or brew in the teapot? China woman, brittle, yet bold as silence. Protect the roof, regret is not an option and refusal works. Escape again. Always escape. Have faith.

The following pieces of writing emerged in different schools from this exercise in which the whole group spontaneously released the words associated with a specific character, and then each student used as many of these words as possible to write without stopping to think. This enabled the same daydreamy quality that informed my first-draft writing of the play to guide their own writing as they reflected upon it. Here they are, in the raw:

> **Ratcatcher** shows the end for some. Separation is what he specialises in. He has always and will always be the one to watch. He never leaves. He is always there. Loneliness. He is a tone and scary, makes you feel alone with his wicked words. The fictional and mythical character, evil demon to Eva as a child. He is the reason for the happenings, the shadow of imagination. Tall, dark, sneaky story character who acts as the danger for Eva's family. He contradicts what Eva feels. He is the shadow of her past, the reason she remembered in an instant. Creepy, spindly, long and stretched he doesn't have a name. The one that makes you wince and shudder: the Ratcatcher.

> **Helga**, nasty victim having to let go of her maternal ways. Decisive but presumptuous. Her loneliness leads to trauma. Although proactive, she is cruel.

> **The Ratcatcher.** In the dead of night the paranoia follows Eva. Scared and fearful, she evades his clasp. Evelyn however is stalked by the shape-shifter. His flickering candlelit shadow reveals crooked, living nightmare. The fiction engulfed her. The looming shadow passes over her like a blanket. Ghostly figure. Twisted murderer follows his prey, glides above cobbles. Eternal pain. Everlasting fear drains life from victims, controlling them. A doctor for dead souls. Blood-red stains a white lab coat. He leads Eva and Evelyn simultaneously through time and generations into his dim lair.

> **Lil** is a welcoming, helpful mother-like figure in Eva's life. She has the warm meaningful desire to help Eva as she guides her through hard times. Separation is a key aspect throughout the play and perhaps when Eva does not get the train to be evacuated the connection between her and Lil

prevails. The bond is critical because even when Eva speaks German, which was a barrier to the Organiser, Lil still understands her.

The Ratcatcher is a threat to Eva throughout her life, an unwanted yet confusing figure, symbolising loneliness, using his deceptive and manipulative ways to steal happiness. He is greedy, wanting everything he sees, a real mysterious, dark figure, lurking in the shadows. Eva feels isolated by the Ratcatcher.

Faith is supposed to be one of the most important things in Evelyn's life, yet she often feels alone and sad while her mother is wallowing in her past. Faith is also embarrassed about her mother's erratic behaviour and habits. When Evelyn starts to ignore Faith's ideas and conversations, Faith has no one else to talk to. So the character who truly is the most alone, is Faith.

The Ratcatcher watches from the shadows with razor eyes, a phantom of myself. He is everything I cannot be. He is consuming me whole. I am haunted by him. His demonic laugh as I fumble and panic. The way he manages to entrap me time and time again in his dark, icy grip. He is not real. He cannot hurt me. But he feels real, like a poison.

Eva craves stability after being neglected by her Jewish mother. Left as a misunderstood outsider. Isolated, lost, confused and weak. A major victim of the ghostly Ratcatcher nightmare. Paranoid of his mythical lurking. Her fragile, innocent and worried thoughts creating barriers from the outer world, eventually creating a strong wall from Jewish life.

A vermin, predator of the night… kidnapping children, yes that's what the Ratcatcher is, stealing children's lives and the joy of growing up. Causing terror amongst young ones and taking away happiness, yes that is his job. Causing separation while hiding in the shadows. He caught Eva and will never be forgotten; he will always be beside her for ever and ever however hard she tries to forget the past. He is the shadow which will never leave sight.

Helga saves Eva, which leaves her lonely. She helps her sew. Regretful. Forgotten about. She has a single-minded approach that things have to be the way she wants them, including her daughter. She's sad. Lonely. She's old, powerless, and unappreciated. But she is unappreciative whilst being strong, easily annoyed and is unable to deal with things at times. New York. She fades out. She is forgotten about, and left to her own devices. She is strong when she's not there. She's weak when she is. Regretful. Helga.

The Ratcatcher was there, well not really there. I just saw a shadow flash across the station floor and for those few split seconds it felt like that shadow had taken away all the happiness. I recognised his long pointed fingernails coming towards me as it went dark and grey. He's tormenting me, murdering my happiness, closing me off in a mousetrap. The door shuts and I can't get out. All I can hear is his hissing and spitting from outside. You can't escape him, or them, for he is in the Guard on the train, the Postman, and in me. He is always there, but not really there, part of me and everyone that we cannot take away. For when we wish someone would just go away, and we feel spiteful or jealous, our bodies shape-shift into the Ratcatcher, even if it is just for a split second, and that is all he needs, a split second, to murder our happiness. Even though he is a myth, just made up, he is in us all, even just a little bit of us and we only show it for a second, he is still in there, somewhere, waiting. You may not even notice he's there, but I do. I see him. Whenever I am scared, he is always there lurking in the shadows. A doctor with a huge needle, that's what he is. You know it's going to hurt, even if it is just for a second. You just wait for that pain to come, as the needle hangs over you. But even though he is haunting, dark and mysterious in his ways, should I fear him, because he is in all of you and me, so how can he be bad, being but not really there?

This creative approach to writing in response to the play can also be employed to inform preparatory work for formal answers to essay questions. So, take an essay question and swiftly write as many words and phrases as possible that it triggers.

> *How effective is the opening to the play?* – button, Mutti, thread, no, attic, 1939, Hamburg, separation, split, *Rattenfänger*, book, bedtime, abyss, help me, no, tomorrow,

night before, nine-year-old, German, time, two places, memory, storybook, hole, lost, going, stay, send away, reluctance, where, danger, Kristallnacht, subtext, practicalities, yes/no, please, refusal...

The words indicate key themes and these can now be used as a reference to develop a considered answer.

Here is an example, from a student's essay in response to this question, in which the language used in the text is explored to reveal how the play's opening works:

Linguistically, the opening of *Kindertransport* is very effective. Within it, Samuels immediately introduces the effect of separation on Evelyn's memory through the phrases 'please' and 'no'. Although the point-blank response is seen by the audience (through dramatic irony) to be symbolic of Helga's desperation for Eva to be able to look after herself, it is also easy for the audience to see how, being one of her last memories of her mother, the young Eva may mistake this answer for a lack of love. Indeed we see later on in the play Samuels shows us that the fragile memory has in fact been eroded away by time and manipulated by Evelyn's experiences when we hear her 'repeat it'; 'What was it? Over and over! Yes, "No!"' It is interesting to note that, although Helga only says 'no' once, Evelyn remembers it as a repeated phrase, which could be seen to illustrate the poignancy of Helga's words for the young Eva. On the other hand, this misconception of Evelyn's could also be seen to demonstrate the idea that Evelyn believes her mother said 'no' to her more than once. Indeed, perhaps not simply using the word 'no', Helga does refuse Eva a lot in phrases such as 'Because you do' and 'There's no later left'. Most poignantly, 'Bedtime is bedtime' could be seen as Samuels showing Helga's ultimate rejection of Eva; she is still sending Eva away on the Kindertransport, saying 'no' to her pleas to stay.

Another student addressed a question about key symbols in the play with an exploration of one single phrase, 'chipped glass', that Evelyn significantly uses just before leaving Faith alone in the attic in Act One, Scene One:

Explore the significance of key symbols and analyse them in relation to meaning.

A glass is a delicate, 'precious' material and is 'ruined for ever' if chipped. A child is 'precious', delicate and is easily damaged or scarred physically as well as psychologically. Once scarred psychologically, as a child, it affects the child's future and the healing process doesn't completely fix the scar. It is still seen, just like the chipped glass. Evelyn is 'still polishing glasses', which is symbolic, after such a long time, of her continuing to hide and try to make herself look 'okay' and 'clean', but, of course, like a 'chipped glass', others will see something is wrong. Evelyn is still scarred from her ordeal of being separated from her family at a young and delicate age and is covering up. However, she is incapable of completely healing it.

There follow two more excerpts from essays in response to questions addressing key themes in *Kindertransport*: religion and culture; mothers and daughters. I have chosen to include these because each student focuses on a specific image, moment or line of dialogue in order to illustrate a greater point about the play as a whole.

Thematically, how does the author present religion and culture in Kindertransport?

Through Faith's reaction to discovering more about her family's religion (and therefore identity), we discover the importance of religion and culture as a theme in *Kindertransport*. Towards the end of the play, when Evelyn has revealed to Faith all she can supposedly remember from her repressed psyche, as an audience we observe Faith asking her mother, 'Am I Jewish then?' From Faith's question we can see that Samuels is presenting religion in this character's eyes as being the key to her true identity and who she is. Technically she is a Jew, as the Jewish religion is passed down through the female line. Evelyn's response further reveals this theme. She says, 'You've been baptised.' Baptismal imagery is a recurring image throughout *Kindertransport*, reflecting anti-Semitic views that the Jewish race is dirty, needs to be cleansed and rid of the sin that is their religion, and therefore arguably their very self, if religion and culture define a person. Through this we could argue the prominence of this theme throughout *Kindertransport*, as Samuels is constantly exposing her audience to the controversy and dispute surrounding each character's religion and identity, specifically shown through this statement as Evelyn almost takes on the role of the Nazis and anti-Semitics regarding her former religion, her former culture, her former self with such grotesque and callous imagery. One could also look at Evelyn's derogatory statement as Samuels showing her audience that, due to the trauma surrounding Evelyn's religion and culture, she is attempting to deny that it was ever a part of her by ridding any trace of Judaism in the female line of her family.

How does Samuels present relations between mothers and daughters in Kindertransport?

Linguistically speaking, Samuels uses a different word for mother to present the differing and changing relationships in *Kindertransport*. For example, at the very beginning of the play, Eva addresses Helga with the word 'Mutti', a German word for 'Mum'. This word not only has connotations of a strong bond between mother and daughter, but the childish innocence of the name also implies Eva's complete dependency on her mother. The fact that the word is in German is used by Samuels to present the idea of this mother/daughter relationship being based on a shared culture and birthplace. However, as the play progresses and Helga and Eva are distanced by time and geography, Eva's word for Helga soon changes to 'my German mother', implying that now Eva has more than one and can separate them only by the geographical positioning; it is at this point in the narrative that Samuels shows Helga and Lil to be equal in Eva's mind. Towards the end of the narrative the audience begins to witness the effect of separation on a mother/daughter relationship, when we hear Eva call Helga 'that German woman'. It is here the audience truly feels the extent of what Eva had to do to deal with her trauma: block out her mother completely. It could say something that now Samuels shows Eva's only way of identifying her mother is through her birthplace; and in the phrase she keeps herself very distant from 'German' and therefore her mother, implying perhaps that she thinks of Germany and her mother as disgusting.

However, just as Helga starts close and ends distantly, Lil is seen in juxtaposition starting as 'Mrs Miller' and ending as 'Mum'. The phrase 'Mrs Miller' is used to represent the formality with which Eva initially regards Lil. This then progresses to 'Mummy Miller'; a phrase that still, with the use of a last name, implies formality, but at the same time has connotations of maternal attraction. The idea that Lil ends up as 'Mum', the Anglicised version of what Helga began as 'Mutti', could be used by Samuels to present the idea that the mother/daughter relationships have switched places in Eva's head, having been warped by time and loss. The fact Evelyn now talks in English to Lil represents she is now just as close to Lil as she was when she spoke German to Helga.

It is also important to refer not only to the language in the script but also to consider what the dramatic form and staging reveal about the relationships between the characters and structural themes:

The use of two pairs of mothers and daughters on stage helps to represent and explore the mother and daughter relationships in *Kindertransport*. It is interesting to note the presence of Helga in the corner of the stage at the beginning of Scene Two. Whilst Evelyn is talking to Faith about her past, it could present the idea that, although they have grown apart over time, Evelyn will always have Helga in the back of her mind and forever be connected to her biological mother; this could be used by Samuels to show that the relationship bond between mother and daughter, no matter how it manifests itself, is eternal. Additionally, the presence of Helga and Eva on stage during a scene where Evelyn and Lil discuss Evelyn's parenting skills could perhaps imply a sense that the way Helga mothered Eva still plays a huge part in how Evelyn mothers Faith; she is desperate to not be as cold to Faith as her memory tells her Helga was to her.

Separation is a key theme in the relationships between mothers and daughters. It is interesting to note that whilst

Helga sends Eva away to be a 'good parent' and keep her child safe, Eva would rather stay with her mother regardless of the cost. This is mirrored in Faith's reluctance to leave Evelyn ('I don't want to go'). This idea forms the crux of the story: whilst a parent will always do the selfless thing and send their child away, the child will always do the selfless thing and want to stay. Here Samuels could present the idea that Lil is not Eva's real mum and will never be, as she is 'selfish' and keeps Eva for herself.

Within *Kindertransport*, Samuels presents both mother and daughter relationships as having strong parallels with each other whilst constantly reminding us, the audience, of the striking differences caused by different situations in which relationships take place.

Frequently Asked Questions

'If you ask me anything I don't know, I'm not going to answer.'
Yogi Berra

'Sometimes questions are more important than answers.'
Nancy Willard

At one post-show question-and-answer session at a London theatre where *Kindertransport* was being performed, the company was asked what they thought would happen next to Faith. The director paused carefully for a moment, then replied, 'Well, what do you think?' Only when the questioner had answered his own question did the director offer a few of her own reflections.

There are no definitive answers, and being an author certainly does not qualify me to tell anyone else what they feel or believe about anything the play contains. So when people write or ask for my view as if it is definitive, I am wary. Still, questions deserve to be addressed. They focus and refocus reflection and stir up perceptions afresh.

So please consider the following enquiries, taken from interviews, emails and letters sent by students, directors, academics, performers, readers and audience members, as an indicator of what people grapple with on encountering the play; and see my replies as personal thoughts rather than the right and only answers.

How do you feel about having your play studied by students?

I think it is fantastic and I hope you really get into it. Use your imagination. I am writer-in-residence at a primary school in London and guided some nine- and ten-year-olds to start working on the play by choosing what they might pack in their case, then enact what it is like to meet a foreign foster family, sharing the first meal with them, what the bed-room room is like, where they are sleeping. They really respond to that.

I encourage those performing or studying the play to draw on their individual experience of parent/child relationships and have confidence in their own interpretation (whilst also paying close attention to the text!). There is an element of mystery that I hope releases your imagination.

Why did you write Kindertransport?

I was very moved by the experience of children who were sent to safety without their parents, and then never got to see them again because they were killed in the Holocaust. I was drawn to their sense of repressed rage that they had been in some way abandoned, even though their lives had been saved. I wanted to explore how people survive traumatic loss and ask if it is possible and how to mend the damage caused by it.

Which scenes do you find to be the most powerful?

Two scenes that always strike me are:

At the beginning – when Helga guides Eva to sew the button onto her coat on her own, teaching her how to look after herself.

At the end – when, as an adult, Evelyn faces Helga at last and tells her that she never wanted to live without her but she was made to do it, and then her mother came back and blamed her for moving away from her.

What was your relationship with your own mother like?

I had struggles with my own mother. We cared for each other very deeply but were very different as people and dealt with difficulty in contrasting ways. It was good to write about a range of different mother/daughter relationships without judging any of the characters. My mother died just before *Kindertransport* opened in the London's West End and it was at once affirming and unnerving to see the play out in public like that not so long after her funeral.

How would you describe your writing?

I am always passionately concerned to explore how people find the courage to face up to their feelings of fear, despair and shame, how we can survive tragedy and disaster without becoming hardened and cruel, remain open and loving.

So my work is about bringing to understanding the darkest realms of the human psyche, fear of annihilation, loss, death, who we dare not be. I am drawn to the mysteries within and connecting these with actual life experience in order to move, inspire and bring us into balance with our light and dark selves, feminine and masculine aspects, without judgement or blame, to find a sense of being whole, individually and collectively.

Are you a feminist?

I was a committed feminist in my teens and early twenties and a piece of that sensibility, a desire for equality, respect and empowerment for women in the world, remains precious to me. I would now describe myself very much as a champion of the feminine voice and archetypal qualities, being true to all aspects of womanliness, (often not always) telling stories with female central characters who grapple with coming fully into their own. I also like creating complex and vital male characters too. My aim is to find balance between the masculine and feminine to find a sense of wholeness.

What do you hope German schoolchildren will understand and take from Kindertransport?

What anyone takes away, which is those deep feelings about loss and parting that we all have, that we can tend to avoid. The performance of *Kindertransport* is an opportunity for people as individuals to sit in a collective space, to experience together something that is very, very private. I would like them to be emotionally touched by what happens to the characters and relate to it in a way that connects with their own lives.

How do you feel about the fact that many students are shocked at the mother/daughter relationship?

Kindertransport probes the painful, hidden side of human nature, tapping into the emotional undercurrents in the shadow of the psyche. Hiding there is the grief, loss and rage that a child feels towards the 'abandoning' mother, no matter how justifiable and understandable her reasons for enforcing separation. Touching on these unnerving and often suppressed feelings is never going to be comfortable, so if anyone responds with shock then I guess the play is working.

I'm a trainee English teacher currently studying Kindertransport *with my Year 12s. We all had a query about the book, and we've all attempted to interpret it, but we're struggling to come up with a secure analysis! The part I'm talking about is when Faith finds all her old dolls in the attic, and they're naked. Could you possibly tell me what the reasoning behind having the dolls naked was?*

When writing a piece of fiction or drama I tend to go with what feels immediate or resonant rather than with what might make sense, so it was an instinct that made me write Faith finding her dolls naked. In interpreting this, it's worth going with what this feels like and translate an emotional or intuitive response into some kind of analysis.

I suppose that there's a sense of these dolls being vulnerable and also reduced to bare essentials. There's also a suggestion of a concentration-camp image, of piles of naked bodies thrown on top of each other, of children being fodder, worthless, discarded like trash. The image is somehow disturbing and needy. This is part of the unconscious state of Evelyn that the play is excavating and which Faith unpacks about her mother.

This play creates metaphorical comparisons without blatantly referring to the subject matter. Was there any particular way in which you decided to include the metaphors in the text?

Metaphors tend to emerge from the unconscious directly onto the page as I write what feels most alive. It is only afterwards that I realise what they might mean, or how there's an image structure through the work. These things can't really be planned, rather they are released and discovered.

Since the play is on some level a universal metaphor for the psychic experience of separation, everything in it must be symbolic of something deeper, invisible and intangible. I guess this is the way I experience life, as a form of poetry, rather than just a literal, physical experience.

I have been so fortunate as to be given the role of Eva for our school play. I was wondering if there is any advice you can offer in regards to characterising the end of Act One, Scene One. In this section, Eva is relieved at reaching the border, but this quickly turns to anger, as she throws down the toffee, etc. I was wondering if this reaction was a result of Eva's own understanding and anger over why she had to leave or a desire to 'join in' with the other, older children, who have perhaps a better understanding of what they have escaped and are celebrating.

Eva's response to crossing the border is a release of tension, all that pent-up fear and rage that she could not vent in Germany because it was far too dangerous to do so. She feels a rush of freedom, no longer has to hold it all together and out it bursts. This is in marked contrast to Evelyn who continues to hold it together for most of the play until, when she at last faces Helga, we see the same rage burst forth at her own mother.

Whilst re-annotating your play, I found myself paying a lot of attention to the inclusion of the German nursery rhyme 'Hoppe, hoppe, Reiter'. As I do German A level, I translated it. The translation I did is quite different to the one included in the play. For instance, the line 'Fressen ihn die Raben' has been translated to 'The Ratman gets you all' instead of 'He will be eaten by the Ravens'. I was just wondering if there was any particular reason was for this, or purely just to make it fit in with the story as most readers will not speak German.

A German speaker translated 'Hoppe, hoppe, Reiter' for the playtext and, as you accurately note, this is a liberal rather than precise translation in order to feed in the Ratcatcher motif and find a rhyme. So please take it with a pinch of salt. The feel and gist is in the spirit of the original adapting it to the themes of the play.

Who are Margaret and Nora? Are they Lil's daughters? Why didn't you go into more depth and detail with them?

Yes, Margaret and Nora are Lil's daughters, both older than Eva. They do not appear as characters in the play because the play deals specifically with aspects of Eva's very particular attachment to Lil. Also, due to theatre budgets, cast size often has to be kept to a minimum. This story has a tight focus.

Would you ever think of making this play into a novel? Was there a purpose of this being a play?

I write plays because I love theatre as a multidimensional art form that works visually, physically, musically and in space. This play can enable a group of people to share very private inner emotions collectively as an audience rather than alone as a sole reader of a novel.

What were your intentions for the play, specifically the purpose of Eva/Evelyn as a character and how the context of the Holocaust influenced your writing?

The Holocaust is the backdrop to this story rather than the theme or focus of it. It was the experience specifically of those on the Kindertransport, being carried away to 'safety' that caught my imagination. In my writing I am drawn to the experiences people have of surviving.

I'm writing to ask you about a line of Kindertransport *that has stimulated lots of discussion. The line is 'Mr Ingratitude. Jesus.' on page sixteen. My students have interpreted this line in several ways: That it refers to Faith's father, that it refers to Jesus Christ, that it could be the Ratcatcher, or perhaps it's Evelyn's father. Could you please clarify this?*

Faith says, 'Mr Ingratitude. Jesus.' because she recognises the name 'Mr Ingratitude' from the story told to her when she was little by her mother. So, 'Jesus' is simply an exclamation of realisation as she starts to make the connection between the German book *Der Rattenfänger* and her own childhood. As yet she doesn't understand what the link is exactly or what it means.

Would it be possible for you to explain what authoritarian influences and figures you used in the play and how their authority is shown?

I am assuming that this is a reference to the Ratcatcher and the various characters he portrays. I would describe the Border Customs Official, English Organiser, Station Guard, etc., as officials rather than authority figures. They do all have uniforms and belong to some kind of state authority, I guess.

The key to the Ratcatcher's connection with these is in Faith's recounting to Evelyn of how she has panic attacks whenever she sees anyone in uniform. This may well stem from Eva's childhood experience in Nazi Germany of seeing Hitler's brownshirts attacking and arresting Jews, and maybe she witnessed such an arrest on Kristallnacht.

Why does Faith use such a strong swear word in Act One, Scene Two?

Faith swears at Evelyn so aggressively at the end of Act One because she is utterly furious with her for not telling her the truth. She is overwhelmed with feeling and this expresses a sense of how important this is to her.

My English class is studying your play, Kindertransport. *I think it is very interesting and enjoyable as it shows the historical background of the Kinder. Is this the only period in time that interests you?*

My plays have been set in the present, in the future, once upon a time after 'happily ever after', in the early nineteenth century, just after the World War One, just after World War Two, during the Spanish Civil War, in the 1960s in the US, in a child's bedroom at bedtime, in the last decade of the twentieth century, in the cave of a prophet, wherever imagination or life might take me.

I often work with people's actual experience and develop stories by adding imaginative dimensions. I also enjoy creating a sense of 'now and forever' in mythical or expressionist worlds that could be anytime or everytime.

I enjoyed your play but didn't quite understand your choice of ending and was wondering if you could explain it to me. Why did we not get to see how their lives turn out?

In the end, Evelyn is able to face up to letting Faith move on and make her own life as an adult. Faith is more able, now knowing the hidden truth, to let go herself. An inner tension has been released.

The shadow of the Ratcatcher means that Evelyn still has to live with her own fears and terrors and maybe she is now more able to do this without trying to pretend that they are not there.

I also wonder what happens in the next phase of their lives. That is another story.

Why use the same actor to play Lil in the past and present?

Lil is a bridge for Evelyn into her experience as Eva and, unlike Evelyn, Lil is not pretending that her younger self never existed. She is in touch with that part that mothered Eva and draws on this in her current life. This is why Lil slips readily between 'now' and 'then'.

Which of the key themes in Kindertransport *is the most important? After narrowing it down to 'separation', 'mother and daughter relationships', 'lack of/change in identity', 'survival', and 'the concept of memory and time lines', I was curious as to what your personal view on this was?*

'Separation' is the key central theme, in my opinion.

How much of this play is meant to be portrayed symbolically as opposed to realistically? It completely changes perspective looking at it from both standpoints.

Kindertransport *is not a naturalistic play but a poetic, heightened piece which employs elements of 'realism' – find the combination of the two that works for you.*

At the end of the play, what gives Eva hope that maybe her mother is a changed woman and will actually be there for her? How come she, for a second, says that she will go with her mother?

I'm guessing that you refer to the scene on the quayside when Helga is setting off for New York and Evelyn doesn't go with her. Eva has agreed to go with her mother because she has felt obliged and pressured to do so and maybe deep down some part of her wants to be able to make this work, but in her heart she wants to stay in England and make her own life, and this takes over when the reality of going becomes imminent. Eva's focus here is not on her mother but on being able to stay where she feels at home. She wants to get away from Helga.

In the last scene between Helga and Evelyn, the language is very heightened, 'I have bled oceans out of my eyes' and, 'You hung me out a window and ripped my soul into shreds.' What is the intention behind this? Is Helga human at this point or is she a memory?

In the final encounter with Helga, Evelyn does not literally meet Helga (who is now dead), rather she faces the 'Helga'/mother part of her own psyche that is as real as any physical form. This is the moment that she admits the inadmissible truth that she has held shamefully within for many years. It is an operatic encounter because this is the voice in her deepest heart that she has always longed and never been able to bear to speak aloud and now, as she does say these words, her inner life and external reality merge at last. There are moments in all our lives that take on epic stature because they are emotional watersheds.

At the end of Act Two, Scene Two, the stage direction is that 'Eva exits'. She does not have a direction to come back on stage but, about a page or two later, the stage direction says that 'Helga and Eva exit'. I am just wondering whether this is a misprint or if it is an option for whoever is directing the play?

Sometimes misprints can happen from edition to edition, especially when this exit was under discussion in rehearsals in an earlier production as it was decided whether Eva is present or not during Evelyn's final encounter with Helga. The repeat of the exit line flags up something of the play's life and possibilities and, although it is an edit that was missed, I like the choice it offers – make your own decision about what you feel works best.

Have you ever watched Kindertransport *and thought, 'I would have done that differently'?*

There is always something that can be changed or improved. If I were to write it today it would be a different play because my approach has evolved and my focus changed, but it feels complete, works well enough and so I'm happy to leave it as it is, flaws and all.

What are your hopes for the play?

I have been moved when people find themselves connecting with their own relationships with their parents and/or children and their experiences of leaving home. It's wonderful when people talk to each other after encountering the play about what they have been emotionally protecting or hiding before. I hope that *Kindertransport* continues its life as a vivid piece of drama that allows many to engage with major events in European and British history in a deeply personal way.

Epilogue

When I wrote *Kindertransport*, I was closer in age to Faith
than to Evelyn. Now I am almost the same age as Evelyn is
in the play. One day, maybe my grandchild, around nine
years old like Eva, will encounter the play and see me on a
par with Lil. In a school recently, the teacher told me that in
her class there were three girls whose mothers had died
within the last few years. They had each responded very
strongly to the play and related their own loss to the experience of this refugee child who came from another culture, era
and place in a time of war.

Life spirals, continually turns back on itself as it goes forward. Do things ever really change? Do we learn from the
experiences of others to do things differently? Or does each
generation experience the same old story, maybe from a different angle, afresh and repeat, repeat, repeat?

How can we connect what happens deep within us, the hidden inheritance from previous generations, the suppressed
fears, with what is happening now in the world around us?

Ruth Barnett, the Kindertransport refugee who has seen the
play many times and who gives talks all around the country,
spent much of her life cutting herself off from her childhood

experience and had no sense of the bigger picture, the events surrounding what had happened to her and her brother.

> I told my children whatever they asked. I left it entirely to them. I didn't hide anything. I cut the feelings off. I knew the story. I knew about the concentration camps. I just didn't want to think about them.

> My brother was in Germany and he wasn't interested. He cut off the past. He never connected it up again. He died three years ago. He tried to make me promise never to talk with his wife or his children. I said, 'Look, you can't put a plaster across my mouth. I promise you that I won't raise the subject, but if they start asking questions I am not going to refuse to answer.' And occasionally they did want to talk about something, and I would simply answer but not volunteer any more. Before he died, when my sister-in-law who had Alzheimer's was decompensating [the return of repressed memories to consciousness], she was very, very distressed at, what I didn't know, that her mother had been a child on the farm in Germany, and the village had been sacked, first of all by the defeated German army who took over the village, kicked them out into the fields, ate up all their food and you can imagine what else they did, and then they had just got back into their homes when the conquering army came and shoved them out again. So she had war memories that she'd never been able to talk about or process. That's what happens when people get older and their mind can no longer keep it repressed. It all comes out. My brother died of a heart attack three weeks after his wife died. So he didn't go through that process of decompensating. It takes a lot of mental energy to keep a trauma repressed, and when your mind gets weaker, if you're old and you have an illness, then you can't any longer keep it repressed and it all comes out. It's like flashbacks, return of the repressed, and then it's re-repressed, it comes out in nightmares, daydreams, flashbacks.

> It's classical that you cope with unbearable things by cutting the feelings off. You know the facts, but so what? And it was not until the Bertha Leverton reunion that I knew anything about the ten thousand children travelling on the Kindertransport. It was not in the public domain

until then. Bertha Leverton put it in the public domain. I really thought that Martin and I were the only two who came over from Germany.

It was a hell of a shock to find so many people all with similar but uniquely different experiences. And they were all telling their stories. I sort of couldn't tell my story. I didn't really know enough about it. But that released something. I had regained my self-esteem. I was a psychotherapist by then. I'd been a relatively successful teacher for nineteen years. I'd raised three children. I had a happy family home and I was ready to take on the past.

In retrospect I realised that every time there was anything to do with the past – for example, Bernie was very interested in the First World War and he would put on war films or read war books – I would have too much ironing to do or something. I didn't even realise how I avoided the past.

I did a lot of catching up very quickly because, two years later in 1991, the government put Holocaust education in the curriculum and the teachers had had no formal education themselves about the Holocaust and yet they were suddenly asked to teach it with no material, no preparation. The LJCC [London Jewish Cultural Centre] was the first organisation to call together a group of people willing to go into schools and help the teachers. So I started to go into schools. I was working full time as a therapist, so I could only go to very local schools, but gradually, when I wound down my practice, I went further and further afield. Now I go all over the country.

I feel very strongly that we haven't learned the lessons of the Holocaust and that we are doomed to repeat it if we don't.

First of all, we haven't got very far in preventing genocide. There have been umpteen genocides since the end of World War Two. We know enough to be able to prevent it. Greg Stanton has created a website called Genocide Watch and he analysed every genocide that has so far been allowed to happen, and they all go through eight stages. Six of these stages take place before the killing begins. If we have the will to stop it, we can. After the killing stops, if we don't bring the perpetrators to justice, if denial is allowed, the genocide doesn't stop, it continues in the eighth stage of denial with no closure until it's fully acknowledged, memorials are set in the killing fields, so that the murdered people are acknowledged and honoured, and then the surviving generations can have closure.

The Armenian genocide is an example of a genocide that is continuing in the eighth stage. Who talks about the Armenian genocide? It provides impunity. Hitler was able to say, 'Who remembers the Armenians? We can do what we like to the Jews and the Gypsies.' That's one aspect. The second is that we have not fully acknowledged the Gypsies. The post-war German government refused to give them victim status until 1982. They continued to call them 'a social nuisance' and wipe them out of the Holocaust, until in 1982 a group of Roma invaded Dachau concentration camp and staged a hunger strike. The government then had to take notice. They then got acknowledgement and some compensation which enabled them to build the Cultural and Documentation Centre in Heidelberg which houses the only permanent exhibition of the Nazi genocide against the Sinti and Roma. I've written a whole book which I'm going to have to publish myself called *Jews and Gypsies: Myths and Realities*. They're the perfect scapegoat and people don't want to let go of their perfect scapegoats. They don't want to leave the comfort zone of their indifference. I'm passionate about the way we treat Gypsies all over Europe.

The Third Reich and World War Two was a breakdown of the male... I don't know what to call it... All the violence was let loose and those who wanted to protect their families were totally unable to do so. I think *Kindertransport* is spot on because it absolutely encapsulates what happens when you have war and persecution, and it's the strengths of the women that enable the human race to survive through catastrophe. Catastrophe is a breakdown of the male function, the masculine function, and the fact that survival is possible is through the female... the female side of men as well... and the masculine side of women... some of the worst camp guards were women. It's the juxtaposition of the masculine and feminine, and the breakdown of the masculine and the efforts of the feminine to hold things together and survive.

As I was completing the first draft of this book, I received the following email from a teacher in the USA:

Ms Samuels,

Hello! My name is Meg Haven and I am currently a high-school drama director, with a BA in Theatre. In college, I played Lil in *Kindertransport*. With the seventy-fifth anniversary of Kristallnacht and the Kindertransport coming up, I wanted terribly to do this show with my students.

It was a huge risk, I knew. These are young kids who have had relatively easy lives. 'How will they ever understand this show?!' I thought. But I decided to be bold and do this play anyway because I felt that it was a story that *must* be told.

Through the rehearsal process, I've done a lot of history lessons with the kids. I have taken rehearsals very slowly so that I can explain what each line means and how the words are cover-ups for what lies underneath. I want to ensure that my kids are telling this story properly.

After our first reading, the kids unanimously agreed that they loved this show! We often do 'easier' shows because of their ability level and they were afraid when I told them this show would challenge them. But after that first reading, they became as passionate as I am about telling this story.

Tonight, after we got through the scene where Evelyn and Helga have their argument ('I wish you had died' / 'I wish you had lived'), the young lady playing Evelyn turned to me and said, 'Wow, Miss Haven! This play is just so... wow! This playwright is a genius!' She was so impressed with the imagery, symbolism, and depth in the show. Her words generated a discussion among the cast about how excited they are to share this story with their audience.

I wanted to pass their words along to you. I consider it a great compliment, coming from modern teenagers. I was petrified they would not understand the seriousness of this era in human history and that they wouldn't treat this story with the reverence it deserves. But they have proven me wrong! They are deeply respectful of the material and recognise what a phenomenal story you have written.

Thank you, so much, for writing this play. I am glad I can share this story and this history with both my students and our audience. You have the highest respect from both me and my students!

It requires courage and integrity to take risks as a teacher and I applaud all those who choose to expand their own and their students' horizons by diving deep into the story, characters and emotional territory of *Kindertransport*. To the theatre-makers, too, who take on the play, I send my respect for rising to the challenge and 'going there'. If it is working, it won't be a comfortable experience, but it does promise to be a worthwhile one, especially if the work is planted very firmly in the present, linking the personal inner experience with what is going on for others, displaced, vilified and separated today, out in the world.

Further Reading

We Came As Children: A Collective Autobiography of Refugees edited by Karen Gershon, 1989, Papermac

Poet Karen Gershon, herself one of the Kinder who travelled to Britain in the late 1930s, edits a series of personal testimonies covering a range of Kinder and follows their journeys and experiences until after the war. The book also contains some of Gershon's moving and eloquent poems about her own experience.

Person of No Nationality: A Story of Childhood Loss and Recovery by Ruth Barnett, 2010, David Paul Press

Berlin-born Ruth Barnett's autobiography portrays her struggle as a Kinder and displaced person to become a British citizen and make a family life and career as a teacher, therapist and educator, raising consciousness about genocide so that the lessons of past atrocities and traumas may be learned to benefit current and future generations.

I Came Alone: The Stories of the Kindertransports edited by Bertha Leverton & Shmuel Lowensohn, 1990, The Book Guild

A range of interviews, letters and testimonies from Kinder who travelled to Britain as child refugees, were housed in foster homes, hostels or schools, and live in adult life as far afield as the United States, Australia and Israel. Poignant and inspiring.

Children's Exodus: A History of the Kindertransport 1938–1948 by Vera K. Fast, 2011, I.B. Tauris

An in-depth look at the people and politics behind the Kindertransport rescue mission, including extracts from interviews, journals and articles, to reveal the experiences and motives of those organising the transportations as well as the children taking part in it.

The Uprooted: A Hitler Legacy by Dorit Bader Whitemen, 1993, Plenum Press

A study of 190 people, including but not exclusively those on the Kindertransport, who escaped the Holocaust, told in their own words. The author also provides psychological insights into the impact of survival.

...And The Policeman Smiled: 10,000 Children Escape from Nazi Europe by Barry Turner, 1990, Bloomsbury

This book traces the story of the Kindertransport and those who helped organise it, drawing on previously unpublished records and extensive interviews. It describes how the Kinder adapted to life in a foreign country including fostering, evacuation and even deportation.

Children's Wartime Diaries: Secret Writing from the Holocaust and World War II by Laurel Holliday, 1995, J Piatkus Books

For a broader perspective, this anthology of diaries gathers writing by children from the ages of ten to eighteen from all over Nazi-occupied Europe. They write of life in the ghettos and concentration camps, of bombings and Blitzkreigs, of fear and courage.

Rosa's Child: The True Story of One Woman's Quest for a Lost Mother and a Vanished Past by Jeremy Josephs with Susi Bechhofer, 1996, I.B. Tauris

One woman's story of how, in her fifties and living in Rugby, England, she discovers the truth about her background and arrival as a three-year-old refugee on the Kindertransport. She then undertakes a quest to find out all she can about her parents and tracks down surviving family members.

Reluctant Refuge: The Story of Asylum in Britain by Edie Friedman & Reva Klein, 2008, The British Library

A perspective on the way refugees coming to Britain are regarded and treated. This book parallels the experiences of, and attitudes towards, forced migrants of the past and present, and argues for a positive and constructive approach to dealing with refugees.

Sophie's Choice by William Styron, 2000, Vintage, Random House

A novel, set in Brooklyn, USA, soon after the war, that evokes the impact of survival on Sophie, a beautiful and fragile Polish Catholic woman who had to make a terrible decision during her time in a concentration camp.

Righteous Gentile: The Story of Raoul Wallenberg, Missing Hero of the Holocaust by John Bierman, 1981, Penguin

An account of the life of Swedish diplomat, Raoul Wallenberg, who saved the lives of tens of thousands of Jews in Hungary at a great personal cost. When the Russians came to liberate Budapest he was taken prisoner and was never heard of or seen again.

Never Again: Britain 1945–1951 by Peter Hennessy, 1993, Jonathan Cape

An overview of Britain after the Second World War – an age of rationing and rebuilding; when hope for a better future contrasted with the horror of conflict and the new, widespread belief that everyone should be treated equally led to the creation of the 'welfare state' and the NHS, despite tough economic circumstances.

The Chief Rabbi's Haggadah by Jonathan Sachs, 2003, Harper Collins

A full rendition, with commentary, of the religious text read as part of Passover festival, telling of the exodus of the Israelites from slavery in Egypt.

Websites and organisations

Genocide Watch – www.genocidewatch.org

Current information on where in the world national, ethnic, racial and religious groups are under threat of attack or annihilation on the grounds of their collective identity. The site aims to raise awareness and enable action to help prevent and halt genocide and related violence.

JCORE (Jewish Council for Racial Equality) – Jewish voice on asylum – www.jcore.org.uk

Website outlining practical campaigns and services for refugees and asylum-seekers in Britain, as well as educational materials to raise awareness about their current and historical experience.

Helen Bamber Foundation – UK-based human rights organisation – www.helenbamber.org

A charity based in London which provides therapeutic care, medical consultation, legal protection and practical support to survivors of human rights violations.

AJR (The Association of Jewish Refugees) – www.ajr.org.uk

Founded in 1941 by Jewish refugees from central Europe, the AJR has extensive experience attending to the needs of Holocaust refugees and survivors who came to this country before, during and after the Second World War. It is also committed to ensuring that future generations can learn about the Holocaust. As well as supporting educational and research projects, the AJR has produced several resources that help perpetuate the legacy of the Jewish refugees and survivors, how they rebuilt their lives and their remarkable contributions to Britain.

Kindertransport group – www.ajr.org.uk/kindertransport

Access to an information pack about the Kindertransport as well as a newsletter for Kinder.

PAGE TO STAGE

Written by established theatre professionals, the volumes in the *Page to Stage* series offer highly accessible guides to the world's best-known plays – from an essentially theatrical perspective.

Unlike fiction and poetry, the natural habitat of the play is not the printed page but the living stage. It is therefore often difficult, when reading a play on the page, to grasp how much the staging can release and enhance its true meaning.

The purpose of this series, *Page to Stage*, is to bring this theatrical perspective into the picture – and apply it to some of the best-known, most performed and most studied plays in our literature. Moreover, the authors of these guides are not only well-known theatre practitioners but also established writers, giving them an unrivalled insight and authority.